Lecture Notes in Computer Science   13861

The series Lecture Notes in Computer Science (LNCS), including its subseries Lecture Notes in Artificial Intelligence (LNAI) and Lecture Notes in Bioinformatics (LNBI), has established itself as a medium for the publication of new developments in computer science and information technology research, teaching, and education.

LNCS enjoys close cooperation with the computer science R & D community, the series counts many renowned academics among its volume editors and paper authors, and collaborates with prestigious societies. Its mission is to serve this international community by providing an invaluable service, mainly focused on the publication of conference and workshop proceedings and postproceedings. LNCS commenced publication in 1973.

Patrick Diehl · Peter Thoman · Hartmut Kaiser ·
Laxmikant Kale
Editors

Asynchronous Many-Task Systems and Applications

First International Workshop, WAMTA 2023
Baton Rouge, LA, USA, February 15–17, 2023
Proceedings

Springer

Editors
Patrick Diehl (iD)
Louisiana State University, CCT
Baton Rouge, LA, USA

Hartmut Kaiser (iD)
Louisiana State University, CCT
Baton Rouge, LA, USA

Peter Thoman
University of Innsbruck
Innsbruck, Austria

Laxmikant Kale
University of Illinois at Urbana-Champaign
Urbana, IL, USA

ISSN 0302-9743 ISSN 1611-3349 (electronic)
Lecture Notes in Computer Science
ISBN 978-3-031-32315-7 ISBN 978-3-031-32316-4 (eBook)
https://doi.org/10.1007/978-3-031-32316-4

This Springer imprint is published by the registered company Springer Nature Switzerland AG
The registered company address is: Gewerbestrasse 11, 6330 Cham, Switzerland

Preface

This volume contains some papers presented at WAMTA 2023, the inaugural edition of the Workshop on Asynchronous Many-Task Systems and Applications, held at the Center for Computation and Technology on the Louisiana State University campus in Baton Rouge, LA, USA, on February 15–17, 2023. The workshop was a hybrid event, with the option for authors and attendees to present, attend and interact both in-person and online.

WAMTA was created in response to the ever-growing scale of high performance computing, and in recognition of the increasing strain this growth puts on software systems at all levels. Core challenges in this context include load-balancing, fast data transfers, and efficient resource utilization. Task-based models and runtime systems have shown that it is possible to address these challenges by providing mechanisms such as oversubscription, task/data locality, shared memory, and data-dependence-driven execution.

The objective of WAMTA is to provide a forum for exploring the advantages and challenges of task-based programming on modern and future HPC systems. It allows developers, users, and proponents of these models and systems to share experience, discuss how they meet the challenges posed by Exascale system architectures, and explore opportunities for increased performance, robustness, productivity, and full-system utilization.

Seven papers were submitted to WAMTA 2023, and the 24 members of the Program Committee (PC) assessed the quality, relevance, and presentation of these contributions. Each paper received at least three reviews by PC members. If the three reviews did not agree, a fourth review was consulted. In the end, a total of six papers were accepted. For each paper, one author in the author list was chosen to present the work. Unfortunately, for one of the accepted papers the authors were not able to present their talk at WAMTA 2023; however, the paper is still included in the proceedings. In addition, some papers represent extended versions of the talks given at WAMTA 2023, including further authors added to the coauthor teams of the accepted papers. The result is six papers of very high quality.

In addition to the presentations of these technical papers, the two and a half day workshop program included three keynote talks, an industrial talk, and 15 technical talks, as well as a poster session.

We would like to thank all authors, speakers, chairs, organizers, PC members and attendees for their contributions towards the success of WAMTA 2023.

Furthermore, we would like to thank our sponsors: Tactical Computing Lab, HPE Enterprise, National Science Foundation, and LSU Center of Computation & Technology.

February 2023   Patrick Diehl
                                                                      Hartmut Kaiser
                                                                      Peter Thoman
                                                                      Laxmikant Kale

Organization

Steering Committee

Patrick Diehl	Louisiana State University, USA
Peter Thoman	University of Innsbruck, Austria
Hartmut Kaiser	Louisiana State University, USA
Laxmikant Kale	University of Illinois at Urbana-Champaign, USA

Program Committee

Jeff Hammond	NVIDIA, USA
Bita Hasheminezhad	NASA Ames Research Center, USA
Pedro Valero Lara	Oak Ridge National Laboratory, USA
H. Metin Aktulga	MSU College of Engineering, USA
Keita Teranishi	Sandia National Laboratories, USA
Weile Wei	Lawrence Berkeley National Laboratory, USA
Brad Richardson	Sourcery Institute, USA
Patricia Grubel	Los Alamos National Laboratory, USA
Kevin Huck	University of Oregon, USA
Dirk Pflüger	University of Stuttgart, Germany
Roman Iakymchuk	Sorbonne Université, France
Huda Ibeid	Intel, USA
Ben Bergen	Los Alamos National Laboratory, USA
Dirk Plciter	KTH Royal Institute of Technology, Sweden
Didem Unat	Koç University, Turkey
Daisy Hollman	Google, USA
Gregor Daiß	University of Stuttgart, Germany
Najoude Nader	Louisiana State University, USA
Sebastian Eibl	Max Planck Computing & Data Facility, Germany
Sebastian Ohlmann	Max Planck Computing & Data Facility, Germany

Sponsors

LSU Center for Computation & Technology
Tactical Computing Lab
HPE Enterprise
National Science Foundation (NSF award 2229751)

Contents

Extending Hedgehog's Dataflow Graphs to Multi-node GPU Architectures

Nitish Shingde[1]([✉])[iD], Martin Berzins[1][iD], Timothy Blattner[2][iD],
Walid Keyrouz[2][iD], and Alexandre Bardakoff[2][iD]

[1] University of Utah, Salt Lake City, UT 84112, USA
{nitish,mb}@sci.utah.edu
[2] National Institute of Standards and Technology, Gaithersburg, MD, USA
{timothy.blattner,walid.keyrouz}@nist.gov,
a.bardakoff@prometheuscomputing.com

Abstract. Asynchronous task-based systems offer the possibility of making it easier to take advantage of scalable heterogeneous architectures. This paper extends the National Institute of Standards and Technology's Hedgehog dataflow graph models, which target a single high-end compute node, to run on a cluster by borrowing aspects of Uintah's cluster-scale task graphs and applying them to a sample implementation of matrix multiplication. These results are compared to implementations using the leading libraries, SLATE and DPLASMA, for illustrative purposes only. The motivation behind this work is to demonstrate that using general purpose high-level abstractions, such as Hedgehog's dataflow graphs, does not negatively impact performance.

Keywords: Hedgehog · multi-node GPU · dataflow · task graphs · Uintah · MPI

1 Introduction

Continuing innovations in hardware pose challenges to developing portable software, particularly for new heterogeneous architectures. These challenges may be addressed by the adoption of new programming models for efficient node use that should represent parallel constructs and make it easier to instrument and reason about an application's performance, thereby allowing developers to gain deeper insight. Two examples of such models are the Hedgehog software [1] and the Uintah Computational Framework [7,16]. Hedgehog specializes in node-level performance and uses C++ threads and NVIDIA CUDA. Uintah specializes in large-scale simulations and uses an MPI+X hybrid parallelism model. Both systems use asynchronous execution to achieve. This paper shows that Hedgehog may be extended by making use of the general philosophy of Uintah. It compares the performance that may be achieved with a prototype version against the well-known DPLASMA and SLATE frameworks. This work builds on the prior work

Supported by organization NIST.

of Holeman [10]; the vehicle for comparison is the well-studied problem of dense matrix-matrix multiplication.

Matrix multiplication performance has improved greatly with the advancement of accelerated devices. Two of the best-known libraries out there that use out-of-core matrix multiplication on multi-GPU accelerated nodes are DPLASMA [5] and SLATE [3]. DPLASMA provides a generic and flexible matrix-matrix multiplication algorithm $C = A \times B$ for multi-GPU accelerated distributed-memory platforms for matrices unrestricted by the size of the GPU memory. The implementation relies on the classical tile-based outer-product algorithm but enhances it with several control dependencies to increase data reuse and optimize communication flow from/to the accelerators within each node. The implementation uses the Parsec runtime system, another task-based runtime system. SLATE is designed to deliver fundamental dense linear algebra capabilities for current and upcoming distributed-memory systems. It is built on top of standards, such as MPI and OpenMP, and de-facto industry solutions, such as NVIDIA CUDA and AMD HIP.

The rest of the paper is organized as follows. Section 2 discusses the various frameworks that deal with multi-GPU distributed-memory platforms. With the matrix multiplication problem as a vehicle, the section discusses how some existing state-of-the-art techniques tackle the situation. Section 3 presents the design principles used to implement matrix multiplication for a multi-GPU accelerated distributed-memory platform. Section 4 discusses the design principles of matrix multiplication using Hedgehog. After describing Hedgehog's single-node multi-GPU solution, the extension to multiple nodes will be given. Section 5 compares Hedgehog's results against those of SLATE and DPLASMA. Section 6 concludes the paper leaving Sect. 7 with possible future plans.

2   Existing Approaches

2.1   Uintah

Part of the original motivation for the extension of the Hedgehog system to multiple nodes is the scalability of asynchronous many-task (AMT) runtime systems and their use in helping manage the increased concurrency, deep memory hierarchies, and heterogeneity. Such runtime systems are advantageous for their ability to handle increasing node-level parallelism through the task overdecomposition of an application while also managing low-level system details necessary for efficient resource utilization behind-the-scenes. Examples include Charm++ [14], HPX [13], Legion [6], PaRSEC [8], and Uintah [7].

While Uintah has demonstrated large scale scalability on heterogeneous architectures [16], it started as a fixed task-graph execution code and was extended to dynamic task execution [15]. Uintah's runtime system manages the asynchronous and out-of-order (where appropriate) execution of these tasks and addresses the complexities of (global) MPI and (per node) thread-based communication. Execution is managed by the task scheduler, which interacts with per-MPI process task queues to select and execute ready tasks (e.g., tasks with satisfied data dependencies). In extending Uintah to heterogeneous architectures, Kokkos [9], was used to meet the challenges posed by diverse heterogeneous systems. Uintah application code then is decomposed into individual tasks that are executed on either the host or device and that make use of Uintah's intermediate portability layer [12], with options to use Kokkos. The resulting tasks are then compiled into a task graph and dynamically executed by the heterogeneous runtime system in an asynchronous out-of-order manner. Scaling capabilities have been shown for two benchmarks using Uintah's MPI+Kokkos scheduler [11] and the accompanying portable abstractions [12] to execute workloads representative of typical Uintah applications. The recent results in [16] at scale shows good strong-scaling to 24,576 NVIDIA V100 GPUs and 8,192 IBM POWER9 processors and demonstrate Uintah's preparedness for the diverse heterogeneous systems accompanying Exascale computing. The key lessons from Uintah for this work are to use separate task graphs per MPI process and to prioritize external communication while hiding its impact using overdecomposition.

2.2 DPLASMA

DPLASMA is a distributed parallel linear algebra software targeted toward multicore architectures. The matrix multiplication algorithm uses the Parameterized Task Grap (PTG), a type of Domain Specific Language (DSL), and exposes it in a compact and problem-size independent format that is queried on-demand to discover data dependencies in a distributed fashion. It depicts algorithms using data flow principles as pure data dependencies between BLAS kernels. The resulting dataflow depiction uses PaRSEC, a state-of-the-art runtime system, to run it in a distributed environment. The algorithm uses several control dependencies like b and c (block sizes for matrix C), d (depth), and l (look-ahead) to increase the data reuses and optimize the communication flow from/to accelerators within each node. It uses cuBLAS's General Matrix Multiplication (GEMM) kernel for computation and MPI for nodal communication.

2.3 SLATE

Software for Linear Algebra Targeting Exascale, also known as SLATE, aims to provide newer linear algebra packages targeting modern many-node HPC clusters. It uses a newer matrix storage format where tiles are the first-class objects, thus leaving the traditional dense linear algebra software like ScaLAPACK, Elemental, and DPLASMA to use contiguous memory to represent the local matrix in each process. SLATE uses a collection of individual tiles to represent the matrices, with no correlation between the tile's position in the matrix versus in memory. SLATE uses MPI for distributed node parallelism, OpenMP for explicit thread parallelism within nodes, implicit thread parallelism within the vendor's node-level BLAS, and SIMD vector instructions for vector parallelism. SLATE relies on explicit dataflow information for communication, where it will broadcast the required tiles to the processes where it is needed. This approach yields a multicore performance of 170 TFLOP/s on 16 nodes and a peak accelerator performance of 339.2 TFLOP/s when processing double-precision matrices [4].

2.4   Hedgehog

Hedgehog [20] is a C++header-only library without any dependencies for developing general purpose coarse-grained parallel algorithms. It targets a heterogeneous single-node compute units with one or multiple CPUs and one or multiple GPUs. Its execution model works without any added scheduler; the inner threads, attached to Hedgehog nodes, are only managed by the operating systems, and execute based on the presence of data.

The Hedgehog nodes are attached with edges representing the flow of data using queues that store unprocessed data. The nodes and edges are structured under the form of a dataflow graph. These nodes are independent persistent entities that accept and produce data. A node starts its execution as soon as input data are available. Because a node can be linked to another node and each of them are living on different threads they form an inherent parallel asynchronous data pipeline. This pipeline is used to get performance: it simplifies parallelizing I/O, data motion, and computation, and It maximizes system utilization by leveraging data streaming. This implementation aims to design portable performing graphs for heterogeneous nodes (e.g., featuring multiple GPUs).

Hedgehog operates with a variety of nodes. Multi-threaded tasks are responsible for doing heavy computation. These tasks form a group, which share the same input and output edges consisting of queues and synchronization contexts. State manager tasks use localized state, which are thread-safe shareable environments, used for data synchronization. A graph is also a node, allowing graph composition and code sharing. This separation of concerns is considered as a first-class citizen as it facilitates the programmability of the library.

Diverse metaprogramming techniques secure the graph by checking its consistency and validity at compile-time. It is also possible to build a compile-time representation of the graph allowing user-defined tests execution on this representation while compiling and consequently modifying the outcome of the compilation.

Bardakoff et al. have demonstrated the performance of this approach with single-node computations in [1]. The Hedgehog LU decomposition with partial pivoting performed on par with the Linear Algebra Package (LAPACK) dgetrf routine compiled with OpenBLAS in multi-threaded mode. For the matrix-multiplication (BLAS-like GEMM routine), running specific matrix sizes, Hedgehog achieves > 95% of theoretical peak across 4 NVIDIA V100 GPUs, outperforming cuBLASMg and cuBLAS-XT baseline libraries.

3   Extending Hedgehog to Multiple Nodes

Hedgehog executes the dataflow graph entirely scheduler-free based on the flow of data. The order in which this execution model passes data to tasks is non-deterministic, relying entirely on the order in which the operating system context switches threads. This out-of-order design is a staple in how Hedgehog obtains performance but poses some design challenges for getting performance on distributed systems. For example, typical MPI programs expect a structured approach that embeds a specific ordering of messages between nodes. Additionally, Hedgehog nodes are designed in its model for non-overlapping usage to achieve a separation of concerns. For instance, the state manager in Hedgehog is a specialized task that manages the state between two or more tasks. We follow the same separation of concerns design and maintain Hedgehog's execution model when augmenting Hedgehog's abstractions to support multi-node scaling with two new specialty tasks: (1) *Sender* and (2) *Receiver* tasks. Similarly to Uintah [7], each node has its own local task graph instead of having a global task graph to manage work across the nodes for scalability. Each of these local graphs contains these two new specialty tasks to establish a form of communication. In Sect. 4 the *Sender* and *Receiver* tasks are implemented for matrix multiplication and deal with point-to-point communication. Though these tasks use MPI underneath as their communication framework, they are designed to be agnostic of such communication models. In the following section, the term *data* will signify data that flow within a local Hedgehog task graph, whereas the term *message* will represent the data that travel across nodes.

3.1 DataPacket

Serialization/deserialization of data converts complex data structures into a byte stream and vice versa. DataPacket has a buffer to help store these byte streams. We define a MatrixTile class that composes and uses the DataPacket class to store the tile's metadata and the two dimensional matrix-tile data for matrix multiplication. By making DataPacket part of the MatrixTile, we use the DataPacket's buffer to store and use the metadata and data directly. This helps circumvent the overhead of allocating a new DataPacket object and copying the serialized bytes from the tile to the DataPacket.

3.2 Sender Task

A *Sender* task processes data from within the graph and sends them to *Receiver* tasks across processes/nodes. The incoming data to the sender task specify the destination node; the sender does not implement any logic to decide where the message should go. In addition to sending the message, it also sends a context ID as metadata. In MPI, this is possible in the form of tags. The context ID helps the receiver task to deduce the type of message. In the case of matrix multiplication, the "output state" feeds the accumulated tile along with the destination node for the Sender task to pack the data into a DataPacket and send it across to the *Receiver* task of the receiving node.

3.3   Receiver Task

Similar to the *Sender* task, the Receiver task registers all possible data types involved in inter-node communication in the form of template parameters. The receiver task is a daemon thread, which polls for any incoming messages without actually receiving the message. The receiver task obtains the context ID from the polling (tags in MPI), deduces the appropriate data type and buffer size, and enqueues an asynchronous receive call for the incoming message. The receiver task periodically checks this queue for any completed received messages, and based on the data type, it deserializes and pushes the data out through the appropriate outgoing edge. These connections are established when adding edges in the graph between the receiver tasks and their endpoints. The Receiver task is defined in this way in order to handle the out-of-order execution and handle spurious sends based on the flow of data within other processes. There is room for improvement in this approach as the daemon becomes a thread that periodically sleeps. One potential optimization will be if a communicator uses a monitor-based implementation when sending/receiving messages. This would allow for the receiving thread to enter into a wait state until a message is incoming.

4   Matrix Multiplication Using Hedgehog

The algorithm implemented here is an extension of the single node setup implemented in Sect. 4.3 of Alexandre's thesis [20]. The thesis explores the algorithm's evolution from CPU only to CPU+GPU to CPU+multiple GPUs using Hedgehog. We briefly revisit the single-node setup and then its subsequent evolution to multiple nodes using the abstractions mentioned in Sect. 3. While the approach used here lays down the general approach to extend Hedgehog to multiple nodes, the communication model used here is hardwired to this case for matrix multiplication. While the peer-to-peer and one-sided communication requirement is more aligned with Hedgehog's design principle, it makes scaling more challenging, which needs to be addressed in future work.

The terms M, N, and K represent the dimensions of the matrices. T represents the tile size, and M_T, N_T, and K_T represent the number of tiles along the M, N, and K dimensions of the matrices, respectively.

4.1   Single-Node Setup

Figure 1 highlights the data and work distribution. Each matching pair of columns and rows from matrices A and B depicts a unit of work per GPU.

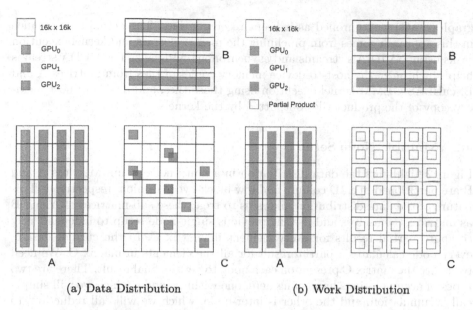

(a) Data Distribution   (b) Work Distribution

Fig. 1. (a) represents the data distribution. For each GPU, only 1 column of tiles from A and 1 row of tiles from B are considered at a time. For matrix C, each GPU gets p partial product tiles (reusable), for storing the partial $GEMM$ computations. (b) represents the work distribution on the GPUs. It is quite similar to the data distribution, where each GPU calculate the partial result for all the elements in matrix C.

The workload is offloaded to each GPU in a round-robin fashion to ensure equal distribution of work. Tiles from matrices A and B are copied to the respective GPUs, where all the tiled-GEMM kernel execution occurs. One thing to note here is that all the GPUs work independently. As we use the outer-product approach, each unit of work asynchronously outputs a partial result for the whole matrix C in the form of tiles. These tiles, called product tiles, are copied back to host memory from the GPU memory for accumulation with matrix C. The accumulation is done on the CPU. There are $M_T * N_T * K_T$ such tile accumulations, i.e., $M * N * \frac{K}{T}$ addition operations in total. It is important to note that the factor $\frac{K}{T}$ here keeps these CPU-side accumulation tasks from being the bottleneck. The GPU memory needs to be large enough to accommodate M_T tiles from a column of matrix A, N_t tiles from a row of matrix B, and 4–8 tiles for storing the product tiles. For detailed information on the Hedgehog data flow graph and its working, refer to Sect. 4.3.1 from Alexandre's thesis [20].

In Hedgehog, the task graph is instantiated only once during its creation. When a task receives new data, the data simply wait in a queue if all the threads concerning the tasks are busy. This differs from traditionally used task graphs in systems like StarPU [18], PLASMA, and CILK [19], where the directed acyclic graph (DAG) gets unrolled as it keeps receiving data. The actual performance in this approach comes from pipelining the memory copies and kernel execution tasks using NVIDIA's streams and asynchronous API calls. The CUDA streams help synchronize the host-to-device memory copies of tiles from matrices A and B, cuBLAS GEMM kernel execution using those tiles, and device-to-host memory copy of the product tiles outputted by the kernels.

4.2 Multiple Node Setup

Figure 2 highlights the data distribution in a multi-node setup. Matrices A and B are partitioned in a 1D column and row block-cyclic fashion, respectively. This nature of the data distribution allows us to treat these sub-matrices of A and B as matrices themselves and use the previous single-node setup to independently compute partial results for every element in matrix C. In the current design, every node calculates a partial result for all the elements in matrix C. We need to reduce the matrix C present on each node to get the final result. There are two types of accumulations happening here, one within a node, which we will simply call accumulation, and the other is inter-node, which we will call reduction, to help distinguish between the two. The cost of reducing matrices is significant and grows as the matrix size and/or the number of nodes increase. The accumulation of matrix C tiles (within a node) happens in stages. So instead of waiting for the whole matrix C to get accumulated, we asynchronously send the accumulated tile as soon as it is ready. Figure 2 depicts the round-robin target distribution of the tiles in matrix C. This distribution of matrix C helps evenly distribute the sends and receives. Using this approach helped spread the communication cost over the execution of the hedgehog graph instead of dealing with a costly singular reduction call. To achieve this asynchronicity, we use the sender and receiver task approach, as detailed in Sect. 3. For the receiver task we had first-hand knowledge of the type of messages and their count from the beginning. Since only 1 type of message was involved, namely, the tiles from matrix C, we could skip the polling step and directly initiate/enqueue an asynchronous receive call.

4.3 Communications

As discussed above, no inter-node communication occurs for matrices A and B. The only communication that takes place is for matrix C. Even with the above asynchronous approach for reducing the matrix C, the communication volume is equivalent to a collective reduction call, which is $M_T * N_T * (n - 1)$ number of tiles, where n is the number of nodes.

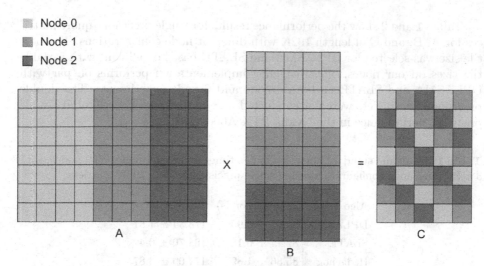

Fig. 2. Data distribution of matrices across multiple nodes. Matrices A and B are distributed in a 1D Block Column and 1D Block Row fashion respectively. Matrix C, as a whole, redundantly resides all the nodes with the ownership marked in 2D Block cyclic fashion.

Within a node, while copying the matrix data to GPU memory, only tiles from matrices A and B are transferred, and that too only once. In total, for a given node, all the $M_T * \frac{K_T}{n}$ tiles from submatrix A, and $N_T * \frac{K_T}{n}$ tiles from submatrix B are transferred from the host memory to the GPU memory. The partial computations are stored in an uninitialized memory in GPU, called product tiles. These product tiles are computed and copied from GPU memory to host for $M_T * N_T * \frac{K_T}{n}$ times. Therefore, the total communication volume, in terms of tiles, to and fro per node is $\frac{K_T}{n}(M_T * N_T + M_T + N_T)$.

5   Results

All the experiments were conducted at CHPC, the Center for High-Performance Computing at the University of Utah. We picked 6 compute nodes, each containing a 64-core AMD third-generation (Milan) 7713P processor. Two nodes consisted of 8 Nvidia RTX A6000 48 GB GPUs per node; the other two nodes consisted of 2 Nvidia A100 80 GB PCIe GPUs per node, and the remaining two nodes consisted of 8 Nvidia A100 80 GB SXM4 per node. The first four nodes had 250 GB of CPU memory, while the last two had 512 GB. Each node had connectX6 HDR Infiniband cards connected with EDR Infiniband. For the 4-node experiment, 3 GPUs per node were used, and for the 6-node experiment, 2 GPUs per node. Both experiments used 12 GPUs in total. Every run is measured over ten iterations and presented as mean and standard deviations of the execution times (seconds) and performances (TFLOP/s).

Tables 1 and 2 show the performance results for single precision square matrices for A, B, and C of length 192K with different node configurations. The best tile size was selected for DPLASMA and SLATE based on all runs with variable tile sizes on our nodes. The Hedgehog implementation performs on par with DPLASMA and SLATE on both 4-node and 6-node experiments. The double precision experiments were not conducted due to the lack of accelerated double precision performance in the Nvidia RTX A6000 GPUs.

Table 1. Mean and standard deviation of run times and performance on 4 nodes, with 3 GPUs per node configuration, using single precision 192K x 192K matrices.

Algo	Time (seconds)	TFLOP/s
DPLASMA	85.23 ± 0.90	178.34 ± 1.87
SLATE	82.74 ± 0.18	183.70 ± 0.42
Hedgehog	85.86 ± 1.89	177.09 ± 3.87

Table 2. Mean and standard deviation of run times and performance on 6 nodes, with 2 GPUs per node configuration, using single precision 192K x 192K matrices.

Algo	Time (seconds)	TFLOP/s
DPLASMA	85.52 ± 0.55	177.73 ± 1.15
SLATE	82.31 ± 0.21	184.64 ± 0.49
Hedgehog	85.92 ± 2.44	177.01 ± 4.77

6 Conclusions

This work aims to extend Hedgehog's abstractions while maintaining its programming model to operate in a cluster environment. We have shown that it is possible to obtain performance in multi-node Hedgehog that is on par with well-known libraries.

The extension of Hedgehog to multiple nodes has been accomplished in a relatively straightforward fashion. The specialized *Sender* and *Receiver* tasks help provide a communication model that aligns with Hedgehog's out-of-order design while remaining agnostic of any particular communication framework like MPI.

There are some caveats with the current approach for matrix multiplication, as it is not yet fully scalable because of redundant copies of matrix C on every node. This implementation also fails to apply proper load balancing for oversubscribed GPUs. The DPLASMA and SLATE libraries outperformed Hedgehog by a margin of 30% and 20%, respectively, when more GPUs were allocated for the same matrix configuration. However, the results are a good starting point for the proposed future work using Hedgehog on more general parallel computing examples.

7   Future Work

The matrix multiplication algorithm could also be tackled by partitioning the work, i.e., focusing on matrix C part by part, like a sliding window. This technique also provides the flexibility to accommodate the possible limitations of GPU and host memory, but at the cost of increased intra-node communication.

One important next step to this work is to add two abstractions to generalize the approach; first, a serialization/deserialization abstraction to our Sender and Receiver task to help deal with complicated data structures; and second, an abstraction for defining decomposition strategies, which can be used to automatically determine where data reside across nodes.

Disclaimer. Certain equipment, instruments, software, or materials, commercial or non-commercial, are identified in this paper in order to specify the experimental procedure adequately. Such identification is not intended to imply recommendation or endorsement of any product or service by NIST, nor is it intended to imply that the materials or equipment identified are necessarily the best available for the purpose.

References

1. Bardakoff, A., Bachelet, B., Blattner, T., Keyrouz, W., Kroiz, G.C., Yon, L.: Hedgehog: understandable scheduler-free heterogeneous asynchronous multithreaded data-flow graphs. In: 2020 IEEE/ACM 3rd Annual Parallel Applications Workshop: Alternatives To MPI+X (PAW-ATM), pp. 1–15 (2020). https://doi.org/10.1109/PAWATM51920.2020.00006
2. Herault, T., Robert, Y., Bosilca, G., Dongarra, J.: Generic matrix multiplication for multi-GPU accelerated distributed-memory platforms over PaRSEC. In: 2019 IEEE/ACM 10th Workshop on Latest Advances in Scalable Algorithms for Large-Scale Systems (ScalA), pp. 33–41 (2019). https://doi.org/10.1109/ScalA49573.2019.00010
3. Kurzak, J., Gates, M., Charara, A., YarKhan, A., Yamazaki, I., Dongarra, J.: Linear systems solvers for distributed-memory machines with GPU accelerators. In: Yahyapour, R. (ed.) Euro-Par 2019. LNCS, vol. 11725, pp. 495–506. Springer, Cham (2019). https://doi.org/10.1007/978-3-030-29400-7_35
4. Gates, M., Kurzak, J., Charara, A., YarKhan, A., Dongarra, J.: SLATE: design of a modern distributed and accelerated linear algebra library. In: Proceedings of the International Conference for High Performance Computing, Networking, Storage and Analysis (SC 2019), Article 26, pp. 1–18. Association for Computing Machinery, New York (2019). https://doi.org/10.1145/3295500.3356223
5. Bosilca, G., et al.: Flexible development of dense linear algebra algorithms on massively parallel architectures with DPLASMA. In: 2011 IEEE International Symposium on Parallel and Distributed Processing Workshops and Phd Forum, pp. 1432–1441 (2011). https://doi.org/10.1109/IPDPS.2011.299
6. Bauer, M., Treichler, S., Slaughter, E., Aiken, A.: Legion: expressing locality and independence with logical regions. In: Proceedings of the International Conference on High Performance Computing, Networking, Storage and Analysis. IEEE Computer Society Press (2012)

7. Berzins, M., et al.: Extending the uintah framework through the petascale modeling of detonation in arrays of high explosive devices. SIAM J. Sci. Comput. **38**(5), 101–122 (2016)
8. Bosilca, G., Bouteiller, A., Danalis, A., Faverge, M., Herault, T., Dongarra, J.J.: PaRSEC: exploiting heterogeneity to enhance scalability. Comput. Sci. Eng. **15**(6), 36–45 (2013)
9. Edwards, H.C., Trott, C.R., Sunderland, D.: Kokkos: enabling manycore performance portability through polymorphic memory access patterns. J. Parallel Distrib. Comput. **74**(12), 3202–3216 (2014)
10. Holmen, J.K., Sahasrabudhe, D., Berzins, M., Bardakoff, A., Blattner, T.J., Keyrouz, W.: Uintah+hedgehog: combining parallelism models for end-to-end large-scale simulation performance. Scientific Computing and Imaging Institute (2021)
11. Holmen, J.K., Sahasrabudhe, D., Berzins, M.: A heterogeneous MPI+PPL task scheduling approach for asynchronous many-task runtime systems. In: Proceedings of the Practice and Experience in Advanced Research Computing 2021 on Sustainability, Success and Impact (PEARC 2021). ACM (2021)
12. Holmen, J.K., Peterson, B., Berzins, M.: An approach for indirectly adopting a performance portability layer in large legacy codes. In: 2nd International Workshop on Performance, Portability, and Productivity in HPC (P3HPC), SC 2019 (2019)
13. Kaiser, H., Heller, T., Adelstein-Lelbach, B., Serio, A., Fey, D.: HPX: a task based programming model in a global address space. In: Proceedings of the 8th International Conference on Partitioned Global Address Space Programming Models (Eugene, OR, USA) (PGAS 2014), Article 6. ACM, New York (2014)
14. Kale, L.V., Krishnan, S.: CHARM++: a portable concurrent object oriented system based on C++. In: Proceedings of the Eighth Annual Conference on Object-oriented Programming Systems, Languages, and Applications (Washington, D.C., USA) (OOPSLA 1993), pp. 91–108. ACM, New York (1993)
15. Meng, Q., Humphrey, A., Berzins, M.: The uintah framework: a unified heterogeneous task scheduling and runtime system. In: Digital Proceedings of The International Conference for High Performance Computing, Networking, Storage and Analysis, SC 2012, WOLFHPC 2012 Workshop, pp. 2441–2448 (2012)
16. Holmen, J.K., Sahasrabudhe, D., Berzins, M.: Porting uintah to heterogeneous systems. In: Proceedings of the Platform for Advanced Scientific Computing Conference (PASC22) Best Paper Award. ACM (2022)
17. Vandevoorde, D., Josuttis, N.M., Gregor, D.: C++ Templates: The Complete Guide, 2nd edn. Addison-Wesley Professional (2017). ISBN 0321714121
18. Augonnet, C., Thibault, S., Namyst, R., Wacrenier, P.-A.: STARPU: a unified platform for task scheduling on heterogeneous multicore architectures. In: Sips, H., Epema, D., Lin, H.-X. (eds.) Euro-Par 2009. LNCS, vol. 5704, pp. 863–874. Springer, Heidelberg (2009). https://doi.org/10.1007/978-3-642-03869-3_80
19. Blumofe, R.D., Leiserson, C.E.: Space-efficient scheduling of multithreaded computations. SIAM J. Comput. **27**(1), 202–229 (1998)
20. Bardakoff, A.: Analysis and Execution of a Data-Flow Graph Explicit Model Using Static Metaprogramming. Université Clermont Auvergne (2021). https://theses.hal.science/tel-03813645

Command Horizons: Coalescing Data Dependencies While Maintaining Asynchronicity

Peter Thoman[✉] and Philip Salzmann

Distributed and Parallel Systems Group, University of Innsbruck,
Technikerstraße 21a, Innsbruck, Austria
{peter.thoman,philip.salzmann}@uibk.ac.at

Abstract. In runtime systems for distributed memory parallel computing which automatically manage dependencies and data transfers, a fundamental trade-off exists between the fidelity of dependency tracking and the overhead incurred by its implementation.

Precise tracking of data state allows for effective scheduling, which can leverage opportunities for compute and transfer parallelism. However, it also induces more overhead, and with some data access patterns this overhead can grow with e.g. the number of iterations of an algorithm.

We present the concept of command horizons, which allow coalescing of previous fine-grained tracking information while maintaining an easily configurable scheduling window with full information precision. Furthermore, they enable consistent cluster-wide decision points without requiring any inter-node communication, and effectively cap the size of state tracking data structures even in the presence of problematic access patterns.

Experimental evaluation on microbenchmarks demonstrates that horizons are effective in keeping the scheduling complexity constant, while their own overhead is negligible – below $10\mu s$ per horizon when building a command graph for 512 GPUs. We additionally demonstrate the performance impact of horizons – as well as their low overhead – on a real-world application.

Keywords: dependency tracking · task graph · asynchronicity · command generation · gpu cluster

1 Introduction and Related Work

Modern high performance computing (HPC) hardware platforms feature many layers of parallelism, memory and communication. While they employ state-of-the-art methods to keep latencies as low as possible, the increase in computational throughput and bandwidth outpaces reductions in latency. Communication latency is thus an important limiting factor for performance, particularly at larger scales. As such, software for HPC systems is frequently designed to leverage asynchronicity as much as possible, enabling e.g. communication and computation overlapping.

© The Author(s), under exclusive license to Springer Nature Switzerland AG 2023
P. Diehl et al. (Eds.): WAMTA 2023, LNCS 13861, pp. 13–26, 2023.
https://doi.org/10.1007/978-3-031-32316-4_2

Developing software which implements these techniques is a challenging endeavor, particularly while relying on the established *de-facto* standard approach to developing distributed GPU applications: "MPI + X", where the Message Passing Interface (MPI) [12] is combined with a data parallel programming model such as OpenMP, CUDA or OpenCL. As a consequence of this complexity, development of new software for HPC is typically left to the select few, and research is often performed using a small set of domain specific software packages.

Parallel Runtime Systems. One promising avenue for improving programmability or enabling more flexible development of and experimentation with high performance code for distributed memory GPU clusters are higher-level *runtime systems*. These typically introduce a broad API and custom terminology, as well as enabling ecosystems of tooling and derived software projects.

A notable example is StarPU [1], an extensible runtime system for programming heterogeneous systems. It offers a wide array of scheduling approaches, from simple FCFS policies, over work-stealing and heuristics, to dedicated schedulers for dense linear algebra on heterogeneous architectures [11,15]. Nevertheless, StarPU's C API is rather low level and requires the explicit handling of data distribution when executing in cluster environments.

Legion [2] is a runtime system designed to make efficient use of heterogeneous hardware through highly configurable and efficient work splitting and mapping to the available resources. Its C++API is intricate and precise, with the explicit intent of putting performance first, before any programmability considerations, making it unsuitable for non-expert users.

HPX [9] is a C++ runtime system for parallel and distributed applications of any scale with a particular focus on enabling asynchronous data transfers and computation. Its heterogeneous compute backend supports targeting both CUDA and SYCL [6].

PaRSEC [3] uses a custom graph representation language called JDF to describe the dataflow of an application [4]. Either automatically generated or written by hand, this representation enables a fully decentralized scheduling model and automatic handling of data dependencies across a distributed system, although the initial distribution of data needs to be provided by the user.

The Celerity programming model [16] was designed to minimally extend the SYCL programming standard [14] while enabling automated distributed memory execution, specifically for clusters of GPU-like accelerators. It asynchronously generates and executes a distributed command graph from an implicit task graph derived from data access patterns.

A related category comprises those projects which extend the grammar of existing programming languages, for example the pragma-based OmpSs [7], or introduce entirely new languages altogether, such as Chapel [5], X10 [8] or Regent [13].

What is clear from this broad and sustained interest is that ways to quickly develop distributed applications and efficiently experiment with different work and data distribution patterns are widely desired. Depending on the level of abstraction targeted by a system, data distribution and synchronization is either manual, semi-automatic or fully automatic.

Tracking Data State. For those systems which transparently manage distributed memory transfers and/or derive their task and command graphs from memory access patterns, *tracking* the state of data in the system at any given point in time is a significant challenge. On the one hand, all opportunities for asynchronous compute and transfer operations should be leveraged, but on the other hand, in an HPC context, scheduling and command generation also need to be sufficiently fast to scale to potentially thousands of cluster nodes.

While for some data access patterns – e.g. stencil-like computations – this is quite manageable with a relatively simple approach, more unusual patterns can present additional difficulties. In particular, as we will outline in more detail in Sect. 2.3, *generative* patterns have the potential to overwhelm data tracking.

In this work, we present *Horizons*, a concept which manifests as a special type of node in task or command graphs for distributed parallel runtime systems. Core design goals and features of Horizons include:

- Maintaining asynchronous command generation and execution.
- Allowing for a configurable tradeoff in the level of detail regarding data state available for command generation.
- Never directly introducing a synchronization point.
- Requiring no additional inter-node communication.

Our implementation of Horizons in the Celerity runtime system achieves all of these goals. Section 2 provides a concise overview of the Celerity system, and describes the type of access patterns which Horizons are particularly effective at managing. Section 3 explains how Horizons are generated, managed and applied, illustrating their impact on command generation. In Sect. 4 we present an in-depth empirical evaluation of the implementation of Horizons in Celerity, including both microbenchmarks and real-world applications. Finally, Sect. 5 concludes the paper.

2   Background

2.1   The Celerity Runtime System

Celerity is a modern, open C++ framework for distributed GPU computing [16]. Built on the SYCL industry standard [14] published by the Khronos Group, it aims to bring SYCL to clusters of GPUs with a minimal set of API extensions. A full overview of the SYCL and Celerity APIs is beyond the scope of this paper[1], so in this section we will focus on how Celerity extends the data parallelism of SYCL kernels to distributed multi-GPU execution, and the data state tracking requirements this induces for the runtime system.

---

[1] Readers may refer to [10,16] and [14], as well as the Celerity documentation at https://celerity.github.io/docs/getting-started.

Listing 1 A basic matrix operation in Celerity.

```
1 distr_queue queue;
2 auto rg = range<2>(512, 512);
3 buffer<float, 2> buf_in(hst_in.data(), rg);
4 buffer<float, 2> buf_out(rg);
5
6 queue.submit([=](handler& cgh) {
7   accessor in{buf_in, cgh, access::one_to_one{}, read_only};
8   accessor out{buf_out, cgh, access::one_to_one{}, write_only};
9   cgh.parallel_for(rg, [=](item<2> itm) {
10    out[itm] = in[itm] * 2.f;
11  });
12 });
```

A typical SYCL program is centered around *buffers* of data and *kernels* which manipulate them. The latter are wrapped in so-called *command groups* and submitted to a *queue*, which is then processed asynchronously with respect to the host process. Crucially, buffers are more than simple pointers returned by a `malloc`-esque API: they are accessed through so-called *accessors*, which are declared within a command group before a kernel is launched. Upon creating buffer accessors, the user additionally has to declare *how* a buffer will be accessed, i.e., for reading, writing or both. This allows the SYCL runtime to construct a *task graph* based on the dataflow of buffers through kernels.

SYCL – in the same fashion as CUDA and OpenCL – abstracts the concept of a (GPU) hardware thread: it allows users express their programs in terms of linear-looking kernel code, which is invoked on an N-dimensional range of work items. Celerity extends this concept to distributed computation. While Celerity kernels are written in the same way as in SYCL, they can be executed across multiple devices on different nodes, with all resulting data transfers handled completely transparently to the user.

The most fundamental extension to SYCL introduced by Celerity are *range mappers*, functions that provide additional information about how buffers are accessed from a kernel. By evaluating these range mappers on sub-domains of the execution range, the Celerity runtime system infers which parts of a buffer will be read, and which ones will be written – at arbitrary granularity.

Tasks. Listing 1 shows an example of a simple matrix operation implemented in Celerity. To transparently enable asynchronous execution, all compute operations in a Celerity program are invoked by means of a queue object. In the first line of Listing 1, this queue of type `celerity::distr_queue` is created. Subsequently, two two-dimensional buffer objects are created, with the former initialized from some host data `hst_in`.

The central call to `distr_queue::submit` on line 6 submits a command group, which creates a new *task* that will later be scheduled onto one or more GPUs across the given cluster. The index space of this task (the 2D range `rg` in this example) will be split into multiple *chunks* that can be executed by different workers. The provided callback (the kernel code) is subsequently invoked with an index object (`itm`) of corresponding dimensionality, which is used to uniquely identify each kernel thread.

Range Mappers. This program closely resembles a canonical SYCL program, with one important difference: Each constructor for `celerity::accessor` is provided with a *range mapper*, in this case a two-dimensional instance of the `one_to_one` mapper. This particular range mapper indicates that every work item of the 512 × 512 global iteration space accesses exactly one element from `buf_in` and `buf_out` each – precisely at the work item index.

In general, range mappers can be user-defined functions, allowing for a high degree of flexibility, with the included *one-to-one*, *slice*, *neighborhood* and *fixed* range mappers serving only to reduce verbosity in common cases.

Execution Principle. The actual execution of Celerity program involves three major steps, each of which proceeds asynchronously with the others in a pipelined fashion: *(i)* task graph generation, *(ii)* command graph generation, and *(iii)* execution.

The *task graph* encapsulates the behaviour of the program at a high level. Essentially, every submission on the queue is represented by a task, and dependencies are computed based on each task's accessor specification. In the lower-level *command graph*, task executions are split up for each GPU, and the required commands for transfers are also generated. Therefore, the number of nodes in the command graph is generally larger than the task graph by a factor of at least $O(N)$. These commands are finally executed on a set of parallel execution lanes.

Summary. While Celerity can be considered a task-based runtime system, its default mode of operation differs significantly from the more common approach taken, particularly in distributed memory settings. Instead of leaving the choice of how to split work or data fully or partially to the user, the Celerity approach is to consider each data-parallel computation as a single *splittable* task. The runtime system is provided with sufficient information, primarily by means of accessors and their associated range mappers, to split these tasks in various ways and distribute them across the cluster.

2.2   Data State Tracking

From a theoretical point of view (in practice, custom acceleration data structures are employed), the runtime system has to track the state of each individual data element, in order to be able to build a data dependence graph and construct the necessary transfer commands. These data structures – one for each buffer managed by the runtime system – track the last operation which wrote to any particular data element. As such, they need to be updated for each write operation performed by a program, and are queried whenever a buffer is read, and the performance of these operations is crucial to the overall efficiency of the runtime system.

For data access patterns common in many physical simulations and linear algebra, the number of individual regions which need to be tracked generally scales with the number of GPUs in the system, as all elements are replaced in each successive time step or iteration of the algorithm. In these cases, *distributed command graph generation*, which only locally tracks the perspective on the total system state which is required for the operations on one node, is highly effective and can scale up to thousands of GPUs. However, it can not mitigate tracking data structure growth with some more complex access patterns.

2.3   Generative Data Access Patterns

In some domains, data access patterns iteratively generate new data over the execution of a program, and might refer to all the generated data in some subsequent computations. We call these access patterns *generative*, and they present a unique challenge for data state tracking.

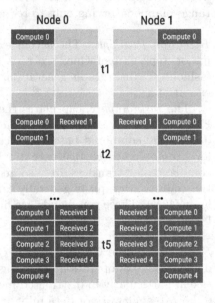

Figure 1 illustrates the state of the tracking data structure of a 2D buffer with a generative data access pattern running on two nodes, after one, two and 5 time steps. In this example pattern, every time step one row of the buffer is generated in parallel, and every subsequent time step requires all previously computed data. For this example, we assume a static 50:50 split in computation between the two participating nodes. As such, after timestep t1, each node will push its computed data to the other in order to perform the computation at t2, and so forth.

Fig. 1. State tracking with a generative access pattern.

With N GPUs, this means that the tracking data structure will contain $O(N*t)$ separate last writer regions at time step t. Even with a highly efficient data structure, the time to query the full previously computed area (e.g. all rows up to $t-1$) will thus scale linearly with the number of time steps.

A simple solution to this particular problem might appear to be to only track whether some data is available locally or on some other node, rather than precise information on which command will have generated it. While this would result in a functionally correct execution, it also implies a complete sequentialization of the command graph up to the most recent data transfer. This would prevent e.g. automatic communication and computation overlapping, the asynchronous sending or receiving of many separate data chunks, or the parallel execution of several independent kernels accessing the same buffers. Horizons provide an elegant solution to this dilemma.

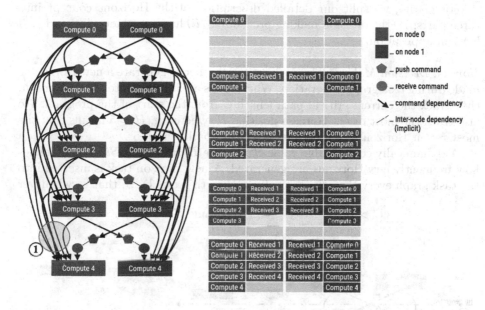

Fig. 2. Command graph and buffer tracking for a generative data pattern.

3   Horizons

Figure 2 illustrates a simplified view of the command graph generated for the first five iterations of a computation with a basic generative data pattern (see Sect. 2.3) scheduled on two nodes/GPUs. It includes compute commands, as well as data push and receive commands. As each row of the involved data buffer is generated by subsequent time steps, the number of dependencies in the command graph scales with the iteration count, as indicated in the figure at location ①.

Horizons solve this issue by selectively coalescing data structures and dependencies, asynchronously and with a configurable level of detail being maintained. From a high-level point of view,"Horizons" describe synchronization points during the execution of a program, in both the task and command graph.

However, it is crucial to note that *no single horizon implies full and immediate synchronization*. Instead, at any point during the scheduling and command generation for a program (after the startup phase), two relevant Horizons exist: the older of the two is the most recent Horizon which was *applied*, which means that all tracking data related to commands scheduled before it was subsumed and coalesced; the newer of the two is the most recent Horizon to be *generated* – it will eventually be applied, but as of now it imposes no synchronization.

As such, the window between the applied Horizon and the current execution front maintains all opportunities for parallel and asynchronous execution and fine-grained scheduling which would be available without Horizons.

For clarity, we split our detailed description of the Horizons concept into three parts: *(i)* the decision making procedure, *(ii)* horizon generation, and *(iii)* horizon application.

Horizon Decision Making. The decision on whether to generate a new Horizon is made during task graph generation. When nodes are inserted into the task graph, they track the current critical path length C from the start of the program. We also track the most recent Horizon position H, where e.g. $H = 5$ means that the most recent Horizon was generated at critical path length 5.

A dynamically configurable value $S > 0$, the *Horizon Step Size*, then defines how frequently new Horizons are generated. A new Horizon task is inserted into the task graph every time the critical path length grows by S, that is, whenever

$$C > H \quad \land \quad (C - H) \mod S \equiv 0 \quad .$$

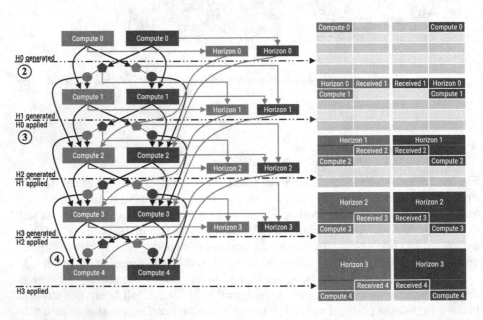

Fig. 3. Command graph and buffer tracking for a generative data pattern with Horizons, using the minimum step size $S = 1$.

Horizon Generation. When command generation encounters a new Horizon task, a corresponding per-node horizon command is generated. This command has a true dependency on each of the nodes in the entire current per-node *execution front* of the command graph, which is easily tracked throughout the command generation process and contains all commands for which there currently are no successors. As a consequence, after each Horizon generation, the execution front contains only the horizon command. Figure 3 shows the generation of Horizon 0 at ② and Horizon 1 at ③. Note that the commands associated with the former only depend on the initial compute commands of each respective node, while all later horizons depend on both the most recent compute and receive commands on their respective node.

Whenever a Horizon is generated for e.g. critical path length C, if a previous Horizon generated for critical path length $C - S$ exists, it is *applied*.

Horizon Application. Applying a Horizon is arguably the most crucial step of the process, as it is what allows for the consolidation of tracking data structures. Crucially, Horizons are always applied with a delay of one step, which maintains fine-grained tracking for the most recent group of commands.

When a given Horizon is applied, all references to previous writers in the tracking data structures which refer to commands preceding the Horizon are updated to instead refer to the Horizon being applied. In the example shown in Fig. 3, at ③ Horizon 0 is applied, thus replacing Compute 0 in the tracking data structures. As such, in any subsequent command generation steps, dependencies which would have been generated referring to any of these prior commands directly will instead refer to the appropriate Horizon. A comparison between ④ in Fig. 3 and ① in Fig. 2 illustrates how Horizons thus maintain a constant command dependency structure with generative data access patterns.

The Horizon approach as presented has the following advantages: *(i)* it is independent of the specifics of the data access pattern, *(ii)* it maintains a constant maximum on the per-node dependencies which need to be tracked, *(iii)* a window of high-fidelity dependency information is maintained, and the size of this window can be adjusted by setting the step size S, *(iv)* horizon generation is efficient, as the required information (current critical path length and execution front) can be tracked with a small fixed overhead during the generation of each command, *(v)* horizon application is highly efficient, as due to the numbering scheme of commands a simple integer check suffices (no graph traversal is required), and *(vi)* no additional communication is required.

4   Evaluation

In this section, we present empirical results which illustrate the effectiveness and efficiency of the Horizon approach as it is currently implemented in the Celerity runtime system. We first present microbenchmarks of simple generative data patterns to precisely track the impact of Horizon step sizes on command generation times.

Secondly, we demonstrate that Horizons have negligible overhead at both small and large scales, and can even be beneficial for programs without generative access patterns, using *dry-run* benchmarks. In dry-run mode, the Celerity runtime system performs all the scheduling and command generation work of a

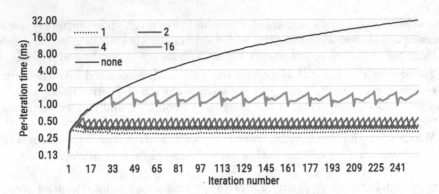

Fig. 4. Per-iteration time for 2D generative access microbenchmark; each line shows a different horizon step setting S (or no Horizons), as indicated in the legend.

real program, but skips the execution of its kernels. This allows us to quickly execute benchmarks on a large – simulated – number of nodes and observe the impact of various optimizations and data structure choices on task and command graph generation performance, without occupying a large-scale HPC cluster.

Finally, we show the impact of Horizons on a full run of a real-world application in room response simulation, which exhibits a generative access pattern.

The hardware and software stack for the microbenchmarks and dry-run benchmarks comprises a single node featuring an AMD Threadripper TR-2920X CPU, running Ubuntu Linux 22.04. As the dry-run benchmarks need no additional hardware and are relatively quick to complete, 30 runs of each configuration were performed and the median result is reported. The real-world application benchmarks were performed on the Marconi-100 supercomputer[2] at CINECA in Bologna, Italy, with 5 runs each.

Microbenchmarks. Figure 4 shows the per-iteration time spent on command generation for a cluster of 512 GPUs, in a microbenchmark of a 2D generative access pattern, with different Horizon configurations. Note that this plot is logarithmic in the Y axis, to better capture the differences between the settings.

Without Horizons (the solid black line), the command generation overhead grows with each iteration of the benchmark, as expected due to the growth of dependencies outlined in Section 3. With a Horizon step size of 16, a drop in overhead is seen for the first time in iteration 33, as the Horizon generated after iteration 16 was applied in iteration 32. The same pattern is visible for the smaller step sizes 4 and 2, but at a smaller scale. With step size 1, the per-iteration time is almost entirely flat.

Figure 5 illustrates the total execution time (blue diamond, left axis) and total time spent on horizon generation and application (green triangle, right axis) of the same microbenchmark. Besides the remarkable decrease in the overall benchmark runtime due to Horizons, which matches the per-iteration results,

---

[2] https://www.top500.org/system/179845/.

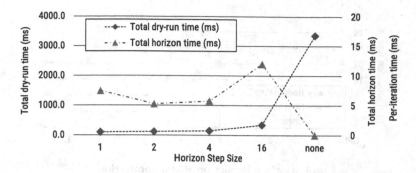

Fig. 5. Total times for 2D generative access microbenchmark.

the behaviour of the Horizon overhead is interesting: when generating a Horizon every time step, the overhead is slightly higher, then it drops, but increases again at $S = 16$. This result can be explained by the fact that, although Horizons are generated far less frequently, the accumulated complexity in the data tracking structure and command graph after 16 iterations makes Horizon generation significantly more expensive. However, even in this case, the Horizon generation overhead only amounts to a total of 12 ms over 256 iterations.

Overhead. For Horizons to provide a suitable solution for coalescing dependencies in a *general* runtime system, they need to have no significant negative performance impact in applications with non-generative access patterns. Figure 6 summarizes results for two such applications: *WaveSim*, a 2D stencil computation, and *Nbody*, an all-pairs N-body physics simulation.

In the *WaveSim* application, the overall impact of Horizons is negligible: the total dry-run time varies by less than 3 ms with and without Horizon use and with different step sizes, and less than 0.5 ms outside of the extreme Horizon step size setting of $S = 1$. For the *Nbody* benchmark, there is a more notable impact – although it is still minor compared to applications with generative patterns. Two particular results stand out: the horizon overhead at step size 1, and the fact that the introduction of Horizons has a positive overall performance

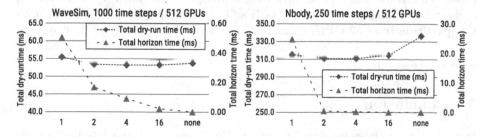

Fig. 6. Horizon impact and overhead for two non-generative applications. X-axis shows Horizon use/step size.

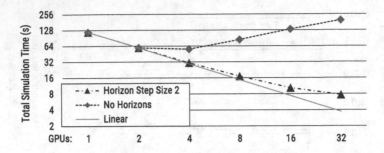

Fig. 7. Horizon impact on RSim application.

impact on the order of 7%. The former is explained by the particular structure of this application, which has two different types of main compute kernels, one of which features only a one-on-one read dependency that can be satisfied locally, while the other requires all-to-all communication. With a Horizon step size of 1, Horizons are inserted after the latter kernel, requiring a much larger number of dependencies. The overall positive impact of Horizons can be explained by their application being utilized to clean up various internal data structures, which can be slightly beneficial even in non-generative cases.

Real-World Application. To confirm the data obtained using microbenchmarking and dry-run experimentation, Fig. 7 shows the result of a strong scaling experiment with the Celerity version of RSim [17], a room response simulation application, over 1000 time steps. RSim computes the spread of a light impulse through a 3D space modeled as a set of triangles. In each time step, the incident light for each triangle depends on the radiosity of all other triangles visible from it, at a point in time that depends on the spatial – and therefore also temporal – distance between the two triangles. As such, the main computational kernel of RSIM exhibits a generative access pattern in which subsequent time steps depend on the per-element radiosity computed in prior time steps.

We compare the current default setting of the Celerity runtime system, Horizon step size 2, with no Horizons. In the latter case, with 4 and more GPUs, command generation overhead starts to dominate the overall simulation run time. With Horizons, near-linear strong scaling is maintained up to 16 GPUs, and strong scaling continues to 32 GPUs. The remaining drop from linear scaling, particularly at 32 GPUs, is not caused by overhead in the runtime system. Instead, it can be attributed to the fact that this is a strong scaling experiment with per-timestep communication requirements.

5   Conclusion

In this paper, we have presented *Command Horizons*, an approach to limiting the data tracking and command generation overhead in data-flow-driven distributed runtime systems with automatic communication, particularly in the presence of generative data access patterns, while maintaining asynchronicity.

Based on their current implementation in the Celerity runtime system, we have demonstrated that Horizons can be generated and applied very efficiently and with low overhead in a variety of applications, and that they are effective at capping command generation overhead at a stable level.

Horizons also have additional applications, e.g. in providing a consistent distributed state for decision making without requiring communication, which we hope to explore in the future.

Acknowledgements. This project has received funding from the European High Performance Computing Joint Undertaking, grant agreement No 956137.

References

1. Augonnet, C., Clet-Ortega, J., Thibault, S., Namyst, R.: Data-aware task scheduling on multi-accelerator based platforms. In: 2010 IEEE 16th International Conference on Parallel and Distributed Systems (2010)
2. Bauer, M., Treichler, S., Slaugther, E., Aiken, A.: Legion: expressing locality and independence with logical regions. In: 2012 International Conference for High Performance Computing, Networking, Storage and Analysis (SC). IEEE (2012)
3. Bosilca, G., Bouteiller, A., Danalis, A., Faverge, M., Herault, T., Dongarra, J.J.: PaRSEC: exploiting heterogeneity to enhance scalability. Comput. Sci. Eng. **15**(6), 36–45 (2013)
4. Bosilca, G., Bouteiller, A., Danalis, A., Herault, T., Lemarinier, P., Dongarra, J.: DAGuE: a generic distributed DAG engine for high performance computing. In: 2011 IEEE International Symposium on Parallel and Distributed Processing Workshops and Phd Forum, pp. 1151–1158 (2011). ISSN 1530-2075
5. Chamberlain, B., Callahan, D., Zima, H.: Parallel programmability and the chapel language. Int. J. High Perform. Comput. Appl. **21**(3), 291–312 (2007)
6. Copik, M., Kaiser, H.: Using SYCL as an implementation framework for HPX. compute. In: Proceedings of the 5th International Workshop on OpenCL, pp. 1–7 (2017)
7. Duran, A., et al.: OmpSs: a proposal for programming heterogeneous multi-core architectures. Parallel Process. Lett. **21**(02), 173–193 (2011)
8. Ebcioglu, K., Saraswat, V., Sarkar, V.: X10: programming for hierarchical parallelism and non-uniform data access. In: Proceedings of the International Workshop on Language Runtimes, OOPSLA, vol. 30. Citeseer (2004)
9. Heller, T., Diehl, P., Byerly, Z., Biddiscombe, J., Kaiser, H.: HPX - an open source C++ standard library for parallelism and concurrency In: Proceedings of OpenSuCo, vol. 5 (2017)
10. Knorr, F., Thoman, P., Fahringer, T.: Declarative data flow in a graph-based distributed memory runtime system. In: International Symposium on High-Level Parallel Programming and Applications (HLPP 2022) (2022)
11. Kumar, S.: Scheduling of dense linear algebra kernels on heterogeneous resources. Ph.D. thesis, Université de Bordeaux (2017)
12. Message Passing Interface Forum: MPI: A Message-Passing Interface Standard, Version 3.1 (2015)

13. Slaughter, E., Lee, W., Treichler, S., Bauer, M., Aiken, A.: Regent: a high-productivity programming language for HPC with logical regions. In: SC 2015: Proceedings of the International Conference for High Performance Computing, Networking, Storage and Analysis, pp. 1–12 (2015). ISSN 2167-4337
14. The Khronos Group: SYCL Specification, Version 2020 Revision 5 (2022)
15. Thibault, S.: On runtime systems for task-based programming on heterogeneous platforms. Thesis, Université de Bordeaux (2018)
16. Thoman, P., Salzmann, P., Cosenza, B., Fahringer, T.: Celerity: high-level C++ for accelerator clusters. In: Yahyapour, R. (ed.) Euro-Par 2019. LNCS, vol. 11725, pp. 291–303. Springer, Cham (2019). https://doi.org/10.1007/978-3-030-29400-7_21
17. Thoman, P., Wippler, M., Hranitzky, R., Gschwandtner, P., Fahringer, T.: Multi-GPU room response simulation with hardware raytracing. Concurr. Comput. Pract. Exp. **34**(4), e6663 (2022)

Shared Memory Parallelism in Modern C++ and HPX

Patrick Diehl[1,2]([⊠])[iD], Steven R. Brandt[1], and Hartmut Kaiser[1][iD]

[1] Center of Computation and Technology, Louisiana State University,
Baton Rouge, USA
{pdiehl,sbrandt,hkaiser}@cct.lsu.edu
[2] Department of Physics and Astronomy, Louisiana State University,
Baton Rouge, USA

Abstract. Parallel programming remains a daunting challenge, from the struggle to express a parallel algorithm without cluttering the underlying synchronous logic, to describing which devices to employ in a calculation, to correctness. Over the years, numerous solutions have arisen, many of them requiring new programming languages, extensions to programming languages, or the addition of pragmas. Support for these various tools and extensions is available to a varying degree. In recent years, the C++ standards committee has worked to refine the language features and libraries needed to support parallel programming on a single computational node. Eventually, all major vendors and compilers will provide robust and performant implementations of these standards. Until then, the HPX library and runtime provides cutting edge implementations of the standards, as well as proposed standards and extensions. Because of these advances, it is now possible to write high performance parallel code without custom extensions to C++. We provide an overview of modern parallel programming in C++, describing the language and library features, and providing brief examples of how to use them.

Keywords: C++ · HPX · parallel libraries and programming language standards · Parallelism

1 Introduction

Parallel programming is an essential part of modern software development and is supported in recent programming languages such as Julia or Rust. However, in older languages such as C++, parallel programming features were not originally included as language or library features. To address this omission, POSIX threads, so-called *pthreads*, a C library, was created for the Unix operating system. The application program interface (API) for pthreads was defined by the *POSIX.1C* thread extension (*IEEE Std 1003.1c-1995*). However, with the C++ 11 standard `std::thread` was added in C++ as a low level interface. At a higher abstraction layer, `std::async` and `std::future` for asynchronous programming were added. In addition, parallel programming utilities, such as smart pointers and lambda

© The Author(s), under exclusive license to Springer Nature Switzerland AG 2023
P. Diehl et al. (Eds.): WAMTA 2023, LNCS 13861, pp. 27–38, 2023.
https://doi.org/10.1007/978-3-031-32316-4_3

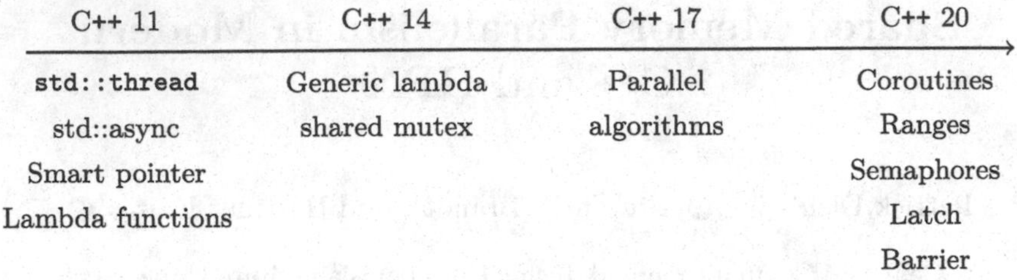

C++ 11	C++ 14	C++ 17	C++ 20
`std::thread`	Generic lambda	Parallel	Coroutines
std::async	shared mutex	algorithms	Ranges
Smart pointer			Semaphores
Lambda functions			Latch
			Barrier

Fig. 1. timeline of the parallel features added to the C++ standard from the beginning of `std::thread` with C++ 11 up to the most recent features of C++ 20.

functions, were added. With the C++ 14 standard, generic lambda functions and shared mutexes were added as utilities. In the C++ 17 standard, parallel algorithms were added. These features allow programmers most of the algorithms added to the C++ 98 standard, *e.g.* `std::sort` or `std::reduce`, to be executed on multiple threads. With the C++ 23 standard, coroutines were added. The keywords `co_return`, `co_yield`, and `co_await` added functionality to suspend and resume functions. Also, in the C++ 23 standard, the *ranges* library was added, which can be seen as the generalization and extension of the algorithm library. Finally, utilities such as semaphores, latch, and barrier were added. In the near future, it is expected that `std::async` will become deprecated to be succeeded by the sender and receiver library (which has yet to be accepted) (Fig. 1).

The C++ standard library for parallelism and concurrency (HPX) implements all the latest features, both proposed and accepted in the C++ standard. In addition, HPX provides extensions to the functionality of the standard, providing mechanisms for distributed parallel programming, alternative ways to create asynchrony, and more.

What is HPX? HPX is an asynchronous many-task runtime system. HPX employs light-weight (user-level) threads that are cooperatively scheduled on top of operating system threads and performs context switches to enable blocked threads to get back to work.

For more details about HPX, we refer to Sect. 3. Because HPX conforms to the C++ standard, any conforming C++ code can be easily converted to HPX code by changing some headers and namespaces. To conclude, while parallelism is included in the C++ standard and no external libraries or language extensions are needed, HPX provides a reliable way to stay on the cutting edge of the standard.

In this paper, we will introduce asynchronous programming, parallel algorithms, and coroutines, senders and receivers (see P2300), and compare the performance between (standard) C++ using operating systems threads and HPX using light-weight threads. Finally, we will discuss the benefits of each approach.

2   Related Work

In the past, parallelism in C++ was usually achieved by using the OpenMP and Cilk as language extensions; Intel Thread Building Blocks (TBB), Microsoft Parallel Patterns Library (PPL) provided access to parallelism through libraries. More recently, Kokkos [3] has provided a library interface to both parallel and heterogeneous computing. While all these approaches have different advantages, they also have different interfaces and none of them are part of the C++ standard. Conforming to the standard might mean that future versions of a conforming code compile and run more reliably, and is one important consideration among many in constructing a new parallel program or adding parallelism to an existing code.

Another longtime player in the asynchronous many-thread library arena is Charm++ [6]. Like HPX, Charm++ also provides facilities for distributed programming (for which, at present, the C++ provides no standard). For a comparison of Charm++ and HPX with OpenMP and MPI (a widely accepted standard for distributed parallel programming) using Task Bench, we refer to [10]. Other notable AMTS are: Chapel [1], X10 [2], and UPC++ [12]. For a more detailed comparison of AMTs, we refer to [9].

3   HPX

HPX [5] is an Asynchronous Many-task Runtime System (AMT) that exposes an ISO C++ standards conforming API for shared memory parallel programming, and extenions to that API library that enable distributed computing. This API enables asynchronous parallel programming through futures, senders and receivers, channels, and other synchronization primitives. This API also eases the burden on a new programmer while learning how to use HPX. It also guarantees application portability in terms of code and performance. HPX employs a user-level threading system that provides a means to fully exploit available parallel resources through fine-grain parallelism on a wide variety of contemporary and emerging high-performance computing architectures. HPX makes it possible to create scalable parallel applications that expose excellent parallel efficiency and high resource utilization. HPX's asynchronous programming model enables intrinsic overlapping of computation and communication, prefers moving work to data over moving data to work, and does so while exposing minimal overheads.

In the context of this paper, we focus on assessing the performance of HPX's implementation of futures and parallel algorithms as mandated by the C++ 17, 20, and 23 standards.

4   Approaches

To showcase the various approaches to shared memory parallelism, we will implement the Taylor series for the natural logarithm in parallel. The Maclaurin series for the natural logarithm ln with the basis e reads as

$$ln(1+x) = \sum_{n=1}^{\infty} (-1)^{n+1} \frac{x^n}{n} = x - \frac{x^2}{2} + \frac{x^3}{3} - \ldots, \text{with } |x| < 1. \qquad (1)$$

For simplicity we will omit the main method and all headers from the code examples. However, we will mention the specific headers in the text, and we provide the complete code for all examples on GitHub®.

4.1 Futures and Futurization

The current abstractions for parallel programming in C++ are low-level threads `std::thread`, `std::async`, and `std::future`. However, in a future C++ standard, it is expected that some of these facilities will become deprecated and will be replaced by sender and receivers. HPX, however, will continue to support an extended version of futures which share many of the capabilities of senders and receivers, including a `then()` method, a `when_all()` method, executors, and so on.

Futures represent a proxy for a result that may not yet be computed and provide a relatively intuitive way to express asynchronous computations. The C++ standard allows programmers to retrieve the value of futures using the `get()` method, but HPX allows programmers to attach a continuation to the future using the `then(std::function<T>)` method. This capability, combined with a `when_all()` method for waiting for future groups, makes it possible to write asynchronous subroutines and algorithms that never block. This is an important consideration for libraries which rely on a pool of workers to carry out parallel computations. Blocking one or more of them might lead not only to slower code, but also blocked code. Routines that are rewritten in this way to run in parallel but without calling `get()` are said to be *futurized*. As of this writing, futurized code is only possible with HPX, and not with the C++ standard.

Listing 1.1 shows the implementation. The amount of work is divided into `num_threads` of partitions with the size `partition_size`. In Line 14, a lambda function is launched to act on each chunk of work asynchronously and an `hpx::future<double>` is returned. Note that we do not need to wait for the lambda function to be finished, and the `for` loop proceeds. This happens because the `hpx::future` is a placeholder for the result of the lambda function, freeing us from the need to wait for it to be computed. In Line 29 a barrier is introduced to collect the partial results using `hpx::when_all`. Here, the HPX runtime waits until all futures are ready, which means that the computation in the lambda function has finished. In Line 30 we specify which lambda function is called. We use the `.get()` function to collect all the partial results. Note that if the result is not ready, HPX would wait here for the result to be ready. However, due to the `hpx::when_all` all results are ready. In Line 36, we need to call `.get()` since `hpx::when_all` returns a future for integration in the asynchronous dependency graph.

Listing 1.1. Parallel implementation of the natural logarithm using `hpx::async` and `hpx::future`.

```
1  double run(size_t n, size_t num_threads, double x) {
2    std::vector<double> parts(n);
3    std::iota(parts.begin(), parts.end(), 1);
4
```

```
5     size_t partition_size = n / num_threads;
6
7     std::vector<hpx::future<double>> futures;
8     for (size_t i = 0; i < num_threads; i++) {
9       size_t begin = i * partition_size;
10      size_t end = (i + 1) * partition_size;
11      if (i == num_threads - 1) end = n;
12
13      hpx::future<double> f = hpx::async(
14          [begin, end, x, &parts]() -> double {
15        std::for_each(parts.begin() + begin,
16                      parts.begin() + end, [x](double& e) {
17          e = std::pow(-1.0, e + 1) * std::pow(x, e) / (e);
18        });
19
20        return hpx::reduce(parts.begin() + begin,
21                           parts.begin() + end, 0.);
22      });
23
24      futures.push_back(std::move(f));
25    }
26
27    double result = 0;
28
29    hpx::when_all(futures)
30        .then([&](auto&& f) {
31          auto futures = f.get();
32
33          for (size_t i = 0; i < futures.size(); i++)
34              result += futures[i].get();
35        })
36        .get();
37
38    return result;
39 }
```

4.2   Coroutines

With C++ 20 coroutines, functions that can be suspended and resumed were added. The three following return types are available for coroutines: co_return which is similar to return, but the function is suspended; co_yield returns the expression to the caller and suspends the current coroutine; and co_await which suspends the coroutine and returns the control to the caller.

A coroutine version of Listing 1.1 can be found in Listing 1.2 In Line 5 of Listing 1.2 we define the function run as our coroutine by having it return an hpx::future. Next, we copied the code from Listing 1.1 for the evaluation of the Taylor series, however, we changed three lines to use the new coroutine features. First, in Line 33, we use co_await while we wait for all futures. Second, in Line 36, we use `co_await` to collect the partial results of all futures. Note in Listing 1.1, we had to call `.get()` here to wait for the futures. Third, in Line 36, we call `co_return` at the end of our coroutine. Note that internally HPX will call `.get()` where we use `co_await`, so the code is easier to read but will not run faster.

Listing 1.2. Example for the computation of the Taylor series for the natural logarithm using HPX's futures and coroutines.

```
1   #include <coroutine>
2
3   hpx::future<double> run(size_t n,
4                           size_t num_threads,
5                           double x) {
6     std::vector<double> parts(n);
7     std::iota(parts.begin(), parts.end(), 1);
8
9     size_t partition_size = n / num_threads;
10
11    std::vector<hpx::future<double>> futures;
12    for (size_t i = 0; i < num_threads; i++) {
13      size_t begin = i * partition_size;
14      size_t end = (i + 1) * partition_size;
15      if (i == num_threads - 1) end = n;
16
17      hpx::future<double> f = hpx::async(
18          [begin, end, x, &parts]() -> double {
19        std::for_each(parts.begin() + begin,
20                      parts.begin() + end, [x](double& e) {
21          e = std::pow(-1.0, e + 1) * std::pow(x, e) / (e);
22        });
23
24        return hpx::reduce(parts.begin() + begin,
25                           parts.begin() + end, 0.);
26      });
27
28      futures.push_back(std::move(f));
29    }
30
31    double result = 0;
32
33    auto futures2 = co_await hpx::when_all(futures);
34
35    for (size_t i = 0; i < futures2.size(); i++)
36      result += co_await futures2[i];
37
38    co_return result;
39  }
```

4.3   Parallel Algorithms

The algorithms within the C++ standard library introduced with the C++ 98 standard were extended with parallel execution in the C++ 17 standard. Listing 1.3 shows the complete code. In Line 14 we use the algorithm `std::for_each` to iterate over each element of the `std::vector` to evaluate the value x of the Taylor series. In Line 20 the algorithm `std::reduce` is used to compute the sum of all evaluations. Note that the only difference between the C++ 98 standard is the first argument of both algorithms, the execution policy. The following execution policies in the header `#include <execution>` are currently available:

- `std::execution::par`: The algorithm is executed in parallel using multiple operating system threads.
- `std::execution::seq`: The algorithm is executed in parallel using one operating system thread.
- `std::execution::par_unseq`: The algorithm is executed in parallel using multiple operating system threads and vectorization for additional optimizations.

Note that this is still an experimental feature and, as of this writing, only the GNU compiler collection (GCC) $\geq$ 9 and Microsoft Visual C++ compiler $\geq$ 15.7 support this feature. Intel's One API compiler uses Thread Building Blocks (TBB) to implement this feature.

Listing 1.3. Implementation of the Taylor series of the natural logarithm using C++ parallel algorithms.

```
1   #include <iostream>
2   #include <future>
3   #include <vector>
4   #include <algorithm>
5   #include <numeric>
6   #include <execution>
7   #include <cmath>
8   double run(size_t n, size_t num_threads, double x) {
9       std::vector<double> parts(n);
10      std::iota(parts.begin(), parts.end(), 1);
11
12      std::for_each(std::execution::par,
13                    parts.begin(),
14                    parts.end(), [x](double& e) {
15          e = std::pow(-1.0, e + 1) * std::pow(x, e) / (e);
16      });
17
18      double result = std::reduce(std::execution::par,
19                                  parts.begin(),
20                                  parts.end(), 0.);
21      return result;
22  }
```

The same functionality for `execution` of parallel algorithms is available within HPX. However, HPX extends the current features available in the C++ 17 standard, allowing execution policies with chunk sizes to specify the amount of each thread is operates on at once. The following chunk sizes are available:

- `hpx::execution::static_chunk_size`: The container elements are divided into pieces of given size and then assigned to the threads.
- `hpx::execution::auto_chunk_size`: Chunk size is determined after 1% of the total container elements were executed.
- `hpx::execution::dynamic_chunk_size`: Dynamically scheduled among the threads and if one thread is done it gets dynamically assigned a new chunk.

For details about the effect of chunk sizes on performance, we refer to [4]. A machine learning approach to determining chunk size is presented here [7,8]. With respect to vectorization, HPX provides the execution policy `hpx::execution::simd` to execute the algorithm using vectorization. In addition, HPX provides a combined execution policy `hpx::execution::par_simd` to combine parallelism and vectorization. Here, `std::experimental:simd` [11], Vc, and Eve are possible backends. Furthermore, HPX's parallel algorithms can be combined with the asynchronous programming. Here, an `hpx::future` is returned and can be integrated into HPX's asynchronous execution graph.

Listing 1.4 shows the usage of the chunk size feature. In Line 4 a static chunk size of ten is defined and passed to the `hpx::for_each` in Line 9 by using `.with()`. In Line 12 the parallel algorithm `hpx::reduce` is wrapped into a future, which can be integrated within HPX's asynchronous dependency graph.

Listing 1.4. Implementation of the Taylor series of the natural logarithm using parallel algorithms.

```
1  #include <hpx/execution/executors/static_chunk_size.hpp>
2
3  double run(size_t n, size_t num_threads, double x) {
4      hpx ::execution ::static_chunk_size scs(10);
5      std::vector<double> parts(n);
6      std::iota(parts.begin(), parts.end(), 1);
7      hpx::for_each(
8          hpx::execution::par.with(scs),
9          parts.begin(), parts.end(),
10         [x](double& e) { e = std::pow(-1.0, e + 1) * std
               ::pow(x, e) / (e); });
11
12     hpx::future<double> f =
13         hpx::reduce(hpx::execution::par(hpx::execution::
               task),
14                         parts.begin(), parts.end(), 0.);
15     return f.get();
16 }
17
18 int main() {
```

```
19    int n = 1000;
20    double x = .1;
21    double result = run(n,10,x);
22    std::cout << "Result is: " << result << std::endl;
23    std::cout << "Difference of Taylor and C\texttt{++} 
         result "
24                << result - std::log1p(x) << " after "
25                << n << " iterations." << std::endl;
26 }
```

4.4   Senders and Receivers

A new framework for writing parallel codes is currently being debated by the C++
standards committee: senders and receivers. One of the goals of this framework is
to make it easier to execute codes on heterogeneous devices. The various devices
are expressed as *schedulers*. In principle, these could be GPUs, different NUMA
domains, or arbitrary groups of cores.

Each step of a calculation is expressed as a *sender*. Senders are typically
chained together using the pipe operator in analogy to the bash shell. Values, error
conditions (exceptions), as well as requests to stop a computation can be carried
through the pipeline.

By default, building the pipeline does nothing. Execution begins only when
ensure_started(), sync_wait(), or start_detached() is called.

Receivers are usually implicit, hidden in the call to sync_wait() at the end.

We note that this proposal was not accepted into the C++ 23 standard, partly
because it was proposed too close to the deadline. It may also need further development. In our experiments writing short codes to use senders and receivers, we
attempted to write a recursive fibonacci routine which took a sender as input and
produced a sender as output and did not itself call sync_wait() to get the result.
In order to write it, we needed to make use of then any_sender<T> class provided
in the HPX implementation but not specified in the standard. Whether additions
of this kind turn out to be necessary, or whether the proposal itself will ultimately
be accepted, remains for the committee to decide.

Listing 1.5. Implementation of the Taylor series of the natural logarithm using sender
and receivers.

```
1  #include <hpx/execution.hpp>
2  #include <hpx/execution/algorithms/sync_wait.hpp>
3  #include <hpx/execution_base/sender.hpp>
4
5  using namespace hpx::execution::experimental;
6
7  template <typename T> concept sender = is_sender_v<T>;
8
9  namespace tt = hpx::this_thread::experimental;
10
11 double run(size_t n, size_t num_threads, double x) {
```

```
12    thread_pool_scheduler sch{};
13
14    size_t partition_size = n/num_threads;
15    std::vector<double> partial_results(partition_size);
16
17    sender auto s = schedule(sch) |
18         bulk( num_threads, [&](auto i) {
19       size_t begin = i * partition_size;
20       size_t end = (i + 1) * partition_size;
21       if ( i == num_threads - 1) end = n;
22       double partial_sum = 0;
23       for(int i=begin; i <= end; i++) {
24          double e = i+1;
25          double term = std::pow(-1.0, e+1) * std::pow(x, e
                )/e;
26          partial_sum += term;
27       }
28       partial_results[i] = partial_sum;
29     }) | then([&]() {
30       double sum = 0;
31       for(int i=0;i<partition_size;i++)
32          sum += partial_results[i];
33       return sum;
34     });
35    auto result = hpx::get<0>(*tt::sync_wait(std::move(s)))
             ;
36    return result;
37  }
38
39  int main() {
40     double x = .1;
41     double r = run(10000,10,x);
42     double a = log(1+x);
43     std::cout << "r=" << r << " " << a<< " => " << fabs(r-a) <<
             std::endl;
```

5   Performance Comparison

For performance measurements on different CPUs, we compiled all examples using gcc 12.1.0 for Arm, using gcc 9.2.0 for AMD and Intel. HPX 1.8.1 was compiled with the following dependencies: boost 1.78.0, hwloc 2.2.0, and jemalloc 5.2.0.

Figure 2 shows the performance obtained for all four of the programming mechanisms presented in this paper for ARM A64FX, AMD EPYC[TM] 7543, and Intel® Xeon® Gold 6140, respectively. To create an artificial work load, we computed the Taylor series in Eq. (1) for $n = 1\,000\,000\,000$. We used perf on the Intel CPU to obtain the floating point operations of $1\,00\,000\,028\,581$ on a single core. For futures using std::future and hpx::future (a), we see that on Arm both implementations perform the same. A similar behavior is obtained for Intel. However, on AMD

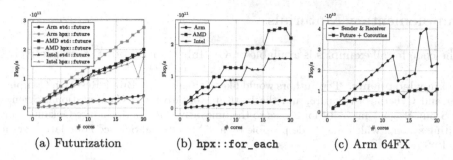

(a) Futurization   (b) `hpx::for_each`   (c) Arm 64FX

Fig. 2. The obtained performance for two concepts for ARM A64FX, AMD EPYC^{TM} 7543, and Intel® Xeon® Gold 6140, respectively. Futurization using `std::future` and `hpx::future` (a) and HPX's parallel algorithm using `hpx::for_each` (b). On Arm64FX coroutines and sender & receiver were tested (c). To create a artificially work load, we computed the Taylor series in Eq. (1) for $n = 1\,000\,000\,000$ and measured $100\,000\,028\,581$ floating point operations using perf on a single Intel core.

`hpx::future` performs better. Here, the overhead of using HPX is negligible. For more details on the overheads of HPX and Charm++, we refer to [10]. For HPX's parallel algorithms using `hpx::for_each` (b), AMD performed better as Intel and Arm is around one order of magnitude slower. Coroutines and sender and receiver were not tested on AMD and Intel since the gcc compiler was too old on the cluster. However, the results on Arm64FX are shown in (c). For the two more recent C++ features, the performance is one order of magnitude slower on Arm than on the two others architectures. Senders and receivers showed the best performance on Arm, however, one should not draw the conclusion that this paradigm is inherently faster from this test.

6   Conclusion

We have shown that Modern C++, through its standard libraries and language features, provides a full and expressive shared memory parallel programming infrastructure for a single node. Therefore, no external libraries or language extensions are necessary to write high-quality parallel C++ applications. We sketched an example of how to use futures, coroutines, and parallel algorithms in the current C++ standard based on a Taylor series code. Furthermore, we provided an introduction to senders and receivers, a framework which might be available in a future C++ standard. For most of these programming mechanisms, we showcased the implementation using the C++ Standard Library using system threads and using the C++ library for concurrency and parallelism (HPX). We did this because HPX provides a cutting-edge implementation of the parallel library proposals being considered by the C++ standards committee.

A performance comparison on a Intel® CPU, AMD CPU, and ARM® A64FX demonstrates that the proposed parallel programming mechanisms do achieve portability of performance without code changes.

Supplementary Materials

The code for all examples is available on GitHub®[1] or Zenodo™[2], respectively.

Acknowledgments. The authors would like to thank Stony Brook Research Computing and Cyberinfrastructure, and the Institute for Advanced Computational Science at Stony Brook University for access to the innovative high-performance Ookami computing system, which was made possible by a $5M National Science Foundation grant (#1927880).

References

1. Chamberlain, B.L., et al.: Parallel programmability and the chapel language. Int. J. High Perform. Comput. Appl. **21**(3), 291–312 (2007)
2. Ebcioglu, K., et al.: X10: programming for hierarchical parallelism and non-uniform data access. In: Proceedings of the International Workshop on Language Runtimes, OOPSLA, vol. 30. Citeseer (2004)
3. Edwards, H.C., et al.: Kokkos: enabling manycore performance portability through polymorphic memory access patterns. J. Parallel Distrib. Comput. **74**(12), 3202–3216 (2014)
4. Grubel, P., et al.: The performance implication of task size for applications on the HPX runtime system. In: 2015 IEEE International Conference on Cluster Computing, pp. 682–689. IEEE (2015)
5. Kaiser, H., et al.: HPX - the C++ standard library for parallelism and concurrency. J. Open Source Softw. **5**(53), 2352 (2020)
6. Kale, L.V., Krishnan, S.: Charm++ a portable concurrent object oriented system based on C++. In: Proceedings of the Eighth Annual Conference on Object-Oriented Programming Systems, Languages, and Applications, pp. 91–108 (1993)
7. Khatami, Z., et al.: HPX smart executors. In: Proceedings of the Third International Workshop on Extreme Scale Programming Models and Middleware, pp. 1–8 (2017)
8. Shirzad, S., et al.: Scheduling optimization of parallel linear algebra algorithms using supervised learning. In: 2019 IEEE/ACM Workshop on Machine Learning in High Performance Computing Environments (MLHPC), pp. 31–43. IEEE (2019)
9. Thoman, P., et al.: A taxonomy of task-based parallel programming technologies for high-performance computing. J. Supercomput. **74**(4), 1422–1434 (2018). https://doi.org/10.1007/s11227-018-2238-4
10. Wu, N., et al.: Quantifying Overheads in Charm++ and HPX using Task Bench (2022). https://doi.org/10.48550/ARXIV.2207.12127
11. Yadav, S., et al.: Parallel SIMD - a policy based solution for free speed-up using C++ data-parallel types. In: 2021 IEEE/ACM 6th International Workshop on Extreme Scale Programming Models and Middleware (ESPM2), pp. 20–29 (2021)
12. Zheng, Y., et al.: UPC++: a PGAS extension for C++. In: 2014 IEEE 28th International Parallel and Distributed Processing Symposium, pp. 1105–1114. IEEE (2014)

---

[1] https://github.com/STEllAR-GROUP/parallelnumericalintegration.
[2] https://zenodo.org/record/7515618.

Framework for Extensible, Asynchronous Task Scheduling (FEATS) in Fortran

Brad Richardson[1]($\boxtimes$) , Damian Rouson[1,2] , Harris Snyder[1] ,
and Robert Singleterry[3]

[1] Archaeologic Inc., Oakland, CA, USA
{brad,damian,harris}@archaeologic.codes
[2] Lawrence Berkeley National Laboratory, Berkeley, CA, USA
rouson@lbl.gov
[3] NASA Langley Research Center, Hampton, VA, USA
robert.c.singleterry@nasa.gov
https://archaeologic.codes, https://www.lbl.gov,
https://www.nasa.gov/langley

Abstract. Most parallel scientific programs contain compiler directives (pragmas) such as those from OpenMP [1], explicit calls to runtime library procedures such as those implementing the Message Passing Interface (MPI) [2], or compiler-specific language extensions such as those provided by CUDA [3]. By contrast, the recent Fortran standards empower developers to express parallel algorithms without directly referencing lower-level parallel programming models [4,5]. Fortran's parallel features place the language within the Partitioned Global Address Space (PGAS) class of programming models. When writing programs that exploit data-parallelism, application developers often find it straightforward to develop custom parallel algorithms. Problems involving complex, heterogeneous, staged calculations, however, pose much greater challenges. Such applications require careful coordination of tasks in a manner that respects dependencies prescribed by a directed acyclic graph. When rolling one's own solution proves difficult, extending a customizable framework becomes attractive. The paper presents the design, implementation, and use of the Framework for Extensible Asynchronous Task Scheduling (FEATS), which we believe to be the first task-scheduling tool written in modern Fortran. We describe the benefits and compromises associated with choosing Fortran as the implementation language, and we propose ways in which future Fortran standards can best support the use case in this paper.

Keywords: Modern Fortran · Task Scheduling · Framework · coarray

1 Introduction

Modern computing hardware has evolved to offer a variety of opportunities to exploit parallelism for high performance – including multicore processors with

© The Author(s), under exclusive license to Springer Nature Switzerland AG 2023
P. Diehl et al. (Eds.): WAMTA 2023, LNCS 13861, pp. 39–51, 2023.
https://doi.org/10.1007/978-3-031-32316-4_4

vector units, superscalar pipelines, and embedded or off-chip graphics processing units. Exploiting the abundance of opportunities for parallel execution requires searching for a variety of forms of parallelism. Chief among the common parallel programming patterns are data parallelism and task parallelism [6]. Parallel programming languages have evolved native features that support data parallelism. In Fortran 2018, for example, such features include giving the programmer the ability to define teams (hierarchical sets) of images (processes) that execute asynchronously with each image having one-sided access to other team members' local portions of "coarray" distributed data structures [4]. These features have now seen use in production codes running at scale for simulating systems ranging from weather [7] and climate [8] to plasma fusion [9].

By contrast, task parallelism generally proves much more challenging for application developers to exploit without deep prior experience in parallel programming. Although data parallelism maps straightforwardly onto a bulk synchronous programming model in which periods of computation are interspersed with periods of communication followed by barrier synchronization, efficient execution of independent tasks generally requires asynchronous execution with more loose forms of coordination such as semaphores. To wit, it takes roughly 15 source lines of code to implement a bulk synchronous "Hello, world!" program using Fortran's barrier synchronization mechanism, the `sync all` statement; whereas it takes more than three times as many lines to write a similar, asynchronous program taking advantage of Fortran's `event_type` derived type, the language's mechanism supporting semaphores [10].

A central challenge in writing asynchronous code to coordinate tasks centers around task parallelism's more irregular execution and communication patterns. Whereas partial differential equation solvers running in a data parallel manner typically involve a predictable set of halo data exchanges between grid partitions at every time step, task parallelism generally enjoys no such regular communication pattern. Programmers generally represent task ordering requirements in a Directed Acyclic Graph (DAG) of task dependencies [11]. Tasks can execute in any order that respects the DAG. Moreover, the DAG can change considerably from one problem to the next and even from one execution to the next. For example, a DAG describing the steps for building a software package will vary over the life of the software as internal and external dependencies change.

Writing code to handle the level of flexibility needed efficiently is daunting for most application developers, which makes the use of a task-scheduling framework attractive. Fortran programmers face the additional challenge that the task scheduling frameworks of which the authors are aware are written in other programming languages such as C++ [12] and UPC++ [13]or target specific domains such as linear algebra [14]. FEATS aims to support standard Fortran 2018 with a standard Fortran 2018 framework and is unique in these aspects.

Rumors of Fortran's demise are greatly exaggerated. Despite longstanding calls for Fortran's retirement [15] and descriptions of Fortran as an "infantile disorder," [16] the world's first widely used high-level programming language continues to see important and significant use. Fortran is arguably enjoying a renaissance characterized by a growing list of new compiler projects over the past several years and a burgeoning community of developers at all career stages writing new libraries [17], including some in very non-traditional areas such as package management [18]. The National Energy Research Scientific Computing Center (NERSC) used system monitoring of runtime library usage to determine that approximately 70% of projects use Fortran [19] and found that the vast majority of projects use MPI.

In MPI, the most advanced way to achieve the aforementioned requirements of loosely coordinated, high levels of asynchronous execution required for efficient task scheduling involves the use of the one-sided `MPI_Put` and `MPI_Get` functions introduced in MPI-3. In the authors' experience, however, the overwhelming majority of parallel MPI applications use MPI's older two-sided communication features, such as the non-blocking `MPI_ISend` and `MPI_IRecv` functions partly due to the challenges of writing one-sided MPI. Our choice to write and support Fortran's native coarray communication mechanism enables us to take advantage of the one-sided MPI built into some compiler's parallel runtime libraries, e.g., in the OpenCoarrays [20] runtime used by `gfortran`, or whatever communication substrate a given compiler offeror chooses to best suit particular hardware. Moreover, this choice implies that switching from one communication substrate to another might require no more than switching compilers or even swapping compiler flags and ultimately empowers scientists and engineers to focus more on the application's science and engineering and less on the computer science.

2   Implementation

FEATS itself consists of eight Fortran modules. Before they can be described, there is one key upstream dependency which must be noted: `dag`, a separate library for manipulating directed acyclic graphs in Fortran. Using `dag`, directed acyclic graphs can be assembled directly in Fortran code, or as a JSON (JavaScript Object Notation) file which is read at run time. FEATS leverages the `dag` library to store the graph of tasks to be executed.

FEATS is designed around the use of Fortran coarrays to provide distributed multiprocessing and data exchange between application images. FEATS automatically assigns the first image to be the "scheduler" image, responsible for tracking what work has been completed and which tasks can be executed next based on the task dependency graph, and assigning work to the other ("compute") images. The `image_m` module provides an `image_t` derived type, which encapsulates the data required for the operation of an image and exposes a single "run" procedure. That run function is given an `application_t` object (provided in the module `application_m`), which stores a list of task objects (described below) and a `dag` graph, which describes the dependencies between tasks.

Tasks in FEATS are represented as objects. FEATS provides an abstract derived type `task_t`, which the user should extend in their own derived type definition, and provide the necessary "execute" function required to complete the task. This design is convenient for the user, but a side-effect is that the tasks will be of different types (granted, with a common base type). Since Fortran does not allow an array to be created where the elements of the array have different types, it was necessary to create a wrapper type, `task_item_t`, which stores a `class(task_t)` as an allocatable member. With this wrapper type, an array of `task_item_t` values can be created and stored. While an implementation detail, in general, a user will not have to interact with `task_item_t` in order to simply *use* FEATS.

Tasks have inputs and outputs, so there must be some mechanism by which to transmit those inputs and outputs between images. This transmission is done using coarrays, though it should be noted that all image control and coarray code is internal to the FEATS library, meaning that the user need not directly deal with any details related to parallel programming, or even understand coarrays. The "execute" function of each task type can accept and return `payload_t` objects, which encode task inputs and outputs. Different tasks will of course have different input and output types based on their purpose, which brings up another difficulty of implementing FEATS as a library. Since the library code cannot know the details of different tasks' input and output types, it must represent these payloads in some generic way so that it can be transmitted between images. FEATS solves the problem by storing payloads as an array of integers (just a string of bytes in memory), and the user must use the Fortran `transfer` statement to serialize their data into and out of payloads. This serialization does come with some caveats; the user needs to ensure that the types they use as payloads can be serialized and deserialized safely (for example, a simple derived type with inline elements will work correctly, whereas one with pointers and allocatable components likely will not). Although arguably an aesthetically "inelegant" approach, the authors see it as an acceptable engineering tradeoff in the interest of generality.

The `mailbox_m` module contains the actual payload coarrays used for data exchange, and the `final_task_m` module contains a task type that serves as a signal to the compute images that all work has been completed. Both of these modules are implementation details, and the user never needs to interact with them directly.

The final module constituting FEATS is `feats_result_map_m`. Tasks, particularly ones at the graph's terminal nodes, may have outputs which the user wants to access after the whole graph has been processed. The aim of the `feats_result_map_m` module is to offer a derived type that tracks which image has the results from terminal nodes in the graph. As of this writing, implementation of the type has not yet been completed. Implementation of such a type should be fairly straightforward, and we plan to add it.

3   Advantages, Disadvantages, and Examples

This section discusses how the features of Fortran enable/support the development of FEATS, and aspects of the language that currently serve as impediments to the desired features of the framework.

3.1   Advantages

There are several features of the modern Fortran language that make it a natural fit for implementing a task scheduling framework. Several aspects have featured prominently in the implementation, but in this section we will discuss what makes them beneficial for implementing a task scheduling framework.

Coarrays and Events. The fundamental problem of task scheduling requires methods of communicating data between tasks, and coordinating the execution of those tasks to enforce prerequisite tasks are completed before subsequent tasks begin. The coarray feature of Fortran provides a simple and effective method of performing one-sided communication between the scheduler and executor images to facilitate data transfer between tasks. While other languages and libraries have methods of communicating data between processes, they often require two-sided operations (i.e. both processes must participate in the communication), require calls to external library procedures, or require significant expertise to use correctly. Having the communication facilities as a native feature of the language simplifies the syntax and implementation complexities and reduces the number of external dependencies.

Although other language and library communication methods are generally sufficient for implementing coordination mechanisms, doing so manually requires a high level of expertise and adds complexity to the implementation. Having a native feature of the language explicitly designed for the purposes of coordination, namely event types, again simplifies the syntax and implementation complexities and reduces the number of external dependencies.

Teams. Although there may be task scheduling algorithms that do not require a reserved process to act as a scheduler, these algorithms generally come at the cost of increased overhead in terms of coordination and complexity of implementation. However, having a dedicated scheduler can introduce a communication and coordination bottleneck in cases of large tasks graphs being executed by large numbers of processes. While we have not yet implemented it, the teams feature of Fortran allows for a simple and natural partitioning of processes such that multiple schedulers can coordinate with segments of executor images operating on partitions of the task graph.

Polymorphism. Although it may be possible to implement a task-scheduling framework without polymorphism, it would require implementation of a predetermined set of possible task interfaces, which would likely be limiting for potential users. By making use of abstract type definitions and type-extension, and defining a generic interface for a task, the procedure of defining a task and including it in a graph becomes a natural process for users, with help from the compiler in enforcing that they have done so properly. The process of defining new tasks involves creating a new derived type which extends from the framework's `task_t` type and providing an implementation for the run procedure. A task can then be created by instantiating an object of this new type, to be included in the dependency graph.

Fortran's History. Fortran's long history of use in scientific computing means that there are likely a large number of applications that could benefit from a Fortran-specific task scheduling framework. We have already identified a potential target application in NASA's OLTARIS [21], space radiation shielding software. Other prime target applications are those which perform a series of different, but long running calculations, or those which perform parallel calculations (or easily could), but which experience load balancing issues.

3.2 Disadvantages

There are some ways in which the Fortran language lacks some important features that would allow for an even better implementation. We will discuss these shortcomings and the ways in which the language could be improved to address them, or how they can be worked around.

Data Communication. The lack of ability to utilize polymorphism in coarrays means that communication of task input and output data cannot be done as seamlessly as users would like. In order to communicate the inputs and outputs between tasks, users are forced to manually serialize and deserialize the data into a pre-defined format for transfer between processes. This means it will also be difficult for users to make use of polymorphism in their calculations, as deserialization of polymorphic objects can be done only with a predefined set of possible result types. Further, the lack of ability to communicate polymorphic objects via coarrays means that each image must have a complete copy of the dependency graph and its tasks, because the tasks themselves cannot be communicated to the executing images later. This represents a moderate inefficiency in data storage and in initial execution for each image to compute/construct the dependency graph. A strategic relaxation of a single constraint in the Fortran standard is all that would be required to enable the use of polymorphism in the data communication.

Task Detection, Fusion or Splitting. Because Fortran lacks any features for introspection or reflection, it is not possible for the framework to automatically detect tasks, fuse small tasks together, or split large tasks apart. All task definition must be performed manually by the user, with no help from the framework. It would be possible to allow users to manually provide information about task and data sizes to encourage certain sequences of tasks to be executed on one image, but would likely be difficult and error prone. Future work could involve exploring avenues for annotating tasks to help the scheduler more efficiently assign tasks to images.

Task Independence. Task independence is a problem for all task based applications, but Fortran provides few avenues for mitigating or catching possible mistakes. Any data dependencies between tasks not stated explicitly in the dependency graph and communicated as arguments to the task or its output allow for the possibility of data races. In other words, all tasks must be pure functions with all dependencies defined. Many existing Fortran applications were not written in this style, and may require extensive work to refactor to a form in which they could take advantage of a task scheduling framework. It is the opinion of the authors that most applications could benefit from such refactoring to enable parallel execution regardless of the desire to use this framework, but understand that the costs involved do not always make this refactoring feasible. Users could make these dependencies explicit without using the framework to transmit the data, but it may be beneficial to develop tools to help users identify these "hidden" dependencies.

Lagging Compiler Support. While the features necessary for developing this framework have been defined by the language standard since 2018, compilers have been slow to implement them, and support is still buggy and lacking. For example, we were able to work around a bug in gfortran/OpenCoarrays regarding access of allocatable components of derived types in a corray on remote images by defining the payload size to be static for the purposes of demonstrating the examples shown below. The other compilers with support for the parallel features have other bugs which have thus far not allowed us to compile and execute the examples with them. Specifically Intel's ifort/ifx has a bug which reports finding duplicate symbols when compiling one of our dependencies. The Numerical Algorithm Group's (NAG) nagfor has a few bugs related to declaring coarrays in submodules. Cray/HPE's Fortran compiler reports mismatches between the interface declared for a procedure in a module and that specified in the submodule, despite the interface not being redeclared in the submodule. We have reported these bugs to those compilers, and are awaiting their resolution to try our framework with them.

3.3 Examples

The examples described in this section can be found in the FEATS repository at https://github.com/sourceryinstitute/feats. In order to give the reader a sense of the compiler landscape, we present one example that is blocked by bugs in current compilers and one example that works correctly with at least one currently available compiler.

A Quadratic Root Finder. The typical algorithm/equation for finding the roots of a quadratic equation can be defined as tasks and FEATS can then be used to perform the calculations. The use of such a simple example can be beneficial for demonstrating the use of the framework. Given a quadratic equation of the form:

$$a * x^2 + b * x + c = 0 \tag{1}$$

then the equation to determine the values of x which satisfy the equation (the roots), is:

$$\frac{-b \pm \sqrt{b^2 - 4 * a * c}}{2 * a} \tag{2}$$

The diagram in Fig. 1 illustrates how this equation can be broken into separate steps and shows the dependencies between them.

The equivalent FEATS application can be constructed as follows, assuming the tasks have been appropriately defined. We also note that the dag library used (and thus the solver object) is capable of producing (and was used to produce nearly exactly) the graphviz source code used to generate the image in Fig. 1.

```
solver = dag_t( &
    [ vertex_t ([integer ::] , "a") &
    , vertex_t ([integer ::] , "b") &
    , vertex_t ([integer ::] , "c") &
    , vertex_t ([2] , "#**2") &
    , vertex_t ([1, 3] , "4*#*#") &
    , vertex_t ([4, 5] , "sqrt(# − #)) &
    , vertex_t ([2, 6] , "−# +− #") &
    , vertex_t ([1] , "2*#") &
    , vertex_t ([8, 7] , "# / #") &
    , vertex_t ([9] , "print roots") &
    ])
tasks = &
    [ task_item_t ( a_t (2.0)) &
    , task_item_t ( b_t (−5.0)) &
    , task_item_t ( c_t (1.0)) &
    , task_item_t ( b_squared_t ()) &
    , task_item_t ( four_ac_t ()) &
    , task_item_t ( square_root_t ()) &
    , task_item_t ( minus_b_pm_square_root_t ()) &
    , task_item_t ( two_a_t ()) &
    , task_item_t ( division_t ()) &
    , task_item_t ( printer_t ()) &
    ]
application = application_t (solver , tasks)
```

This example produces output like the following, with a slightly different order of execution being possible each time except that an operation is never performed prior to the results of the operations on which it depends.

```
c =      1.00000000
b =     −5.00000000
a =      2.00000000
2*a =      4.00000000
b**2 =     −5.00000000
4*a*c =      8.00000000
sqrt (b**2 − 4*a*c) =      4.12310553       −4.12310553
−b +− sqrt (b**2 − 4*a*c) =      9.12310600       0.876894474
(−b +− sqrt (b**2 − 4*a*c)) / (2*a) =      2.28077650       0.219223619
The roots are      2.28077650       0.219223619
```

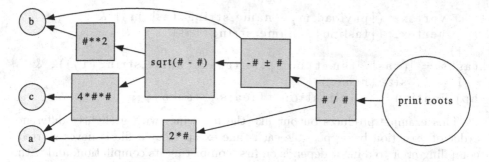

Fig. 1. Graphical representation of the computational tasks involved in calculating the roots of a quadratic equation.

Compiling FEATS. Compiling software projects is a common example of an application involving tasks. By defining the dependencies between files, and defining their compilation as a task, it becomes possible to use FEATS to compile itself. The FEATS source file dependencies are described by the image in Fig. 2, and the FEATS application can be constructed as follows.

```
feats = dag_t(&
  [ vertex_t([integer::], name_string(assert_m)) &
  , vertex_t([integer::], name_string(dag_m)) &
  , vertex_t( &
  [dag_m, task_item_m], name_string(application_m)) &
  , vertex_t( &
  [assert_m, application_m], &
  name_string(application_s)) &
  , vertex_t( &
  [integer::], name_string(feats_result_map_m)) &
  , vertex_t( &
  [payload_m, task_m], name_string(final_task_m)) &
  , vertex_t([final_task_m], name_string(final_task_s)) &
  , vertex_t( &
  [application_m, feats_result_map_m, payload_m], &
  name_string(image_m)) &
  , vertex_t( &
  [dag_m, final_task_m, image_m, &
  mailbox_m, task_item_m], &
  name_string(image_s)) &
  , vertex_t([payload_m], name_string(mailbox_m)) &
  , vertex_t([integer::], name_string(payload_m)) &
  , vertex_t([payload_m], name_string(payload_s)) &
  , vertex_t( &
  [payload_m, task_m], name_string(task_item_m)) &
  , vertex_t([task_item_m], name_string(task_item_s)) &
```

```
, vertex_t ([payload_m], name_string(task_m)) &
, vertex_t ([task_m], name_string(task_s)) &
])
tasks = [(task_item_t(compile_task_t(name_string(i))), &
  i = 1, size(names))]
application = application_t(feats, tasks)
```

This example produces output like the following, with a slightly different order of execution being possible each time except that a file is never started compiling prior to a file it depends on first completing its compilation, and with a possibly different image executing each task.

```
Compiling: dag_m on image number: 3
Compiling: assert_m on image number: 4
Compiling: feats_result_map_m on image number: 2
Finished Compiling: assert_m
Compiling: payload_m on image number: 4
Finished Compiling: dag_m
Finished Compiling: feats_result_map_m
Finished Compiling: payload_m
Compiling: mailbox_m on image number: 4
Compiling: task_m on image number: 2
Compiling: payload_s on image number: 3
Finished Compiling: mailbox_m
Finished Compiling: task_m
Compiling: task_item_m on image number: 2
Finished Compiling: payload_s
Compiling: task_s on image number: 3
Compiling: final_task_m on image number: 4
Finished Compiling: final_task_m
Compiling: final_task_s on image number: 4
Finished Compiling: task_item_m
Compiling: application_m on image number: 2
Finished Compiling: application_m
Compiling: application_s on image number: 2
Finished Compiling: task_s
Compiling: image_m on image number: 3
Finished Compiling: final_task_s
Compiling: task_item_s on image number: 4
Finished Compiling: task_item_s
Finished Compiling: application_s
Finished Compiling: image_m
Compiling: image_s on image number: 4
Finished Compiling: image_s
```

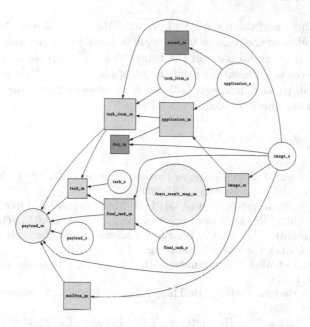

Fig. 2. Graphical representation of the tasks involved in compiling the FEATS library.

4   Conclusion

We believe the existing Fortran applications, and the Fortran ecosystem generally, would greatly benefit from a native tasking framework. The prototype implementation of FEATS has successfully demonstrated that implementing a task scheduling framework in Fortran is feasible. Working around limitations of the language and the bugs in various compilers' coarray feature implementation has proven a challenging but not impassible barrier. With this demonstration of a working prototype implementation, we have taken a significant first step towards providing such a capability to Fortran users.

We look forward to working on several unresolved issues in FEATS. The first order of business will be to implement the `result_map_t` type to allow for further processing of results after completed execution of a task graph. Also, we will submit and follow up on bug reports to the writers of the compilers that we have attempted to use for executing the examples presented. Further, we will begin to explore the performance characteristics of the framework as we use the framework to execute larger task graphs on machines with larger numbers of processors.

Longer term work planned will involve collaborating with the Fortran standard committee to add capabilities to the language that will enable FEATS behaviors such as communication of polymorphic objects between images using coarrays. We have identified a targeted relaxation of a specific constraint in the standard to allow for the needed functionality. We will also explore graph partitioning algorithms and the use of the Fortran 2018 teams feature to potentially improve the ability of the framework to scale to large problems and systems. We also hope to find potential users of the framework and help them to integrate it into their applications. Possible initial target applications include parallel builds with the Fortran package manager [18] and works-stealing with the Intermediate Complexity Atmospheric Research model [8].

References

1. Miguel, H.: Parallel programming in Fortran 95 using OpenMP. Technique report, Universidad Politecnica De Madrid (2002)
2. Message Passing Interface Forum: MPI: A Message-Passing Interface Standard Version 4.0 (2021). https://www.mpi-forum.org/docs/mpi-4.0/mpi40-report.pdf
3. Reutsch, G., Fatica, M.: CUDA Fortran for scientists and engineers: best pracices for efficient CUDA Fortran programming. Elsevier (2013)
4. Numrich, R.: Parallel Programming with Co-Arrays. Chapman and Hall/CRC, Boca Raton (2018)
5. Curcic, M.: Modern Fortran: Building Efficient Parallel Applications. Manning Publications (2021)
6. Massingill, B., Sanders, B., Mattson, T.G.: Patterns for Parallel Programming. Pearson Education, United Kingdom (2004)
7. Mozdzynski, G., Hamrud, M., Wedi, N.: A partitioned global address space implementation of the European centre for medium range weather forecasts integrated forecasting system. Int. J. High Perform. Comput. Appl. **29**(3), 261–273 (2015)
8. Gutmann, E., Barstad, I., Clark, M., Arnold, J., Rasmussen, R.: The intermediate complexity atmospheric research model (ICAR). J. Hydrometeorol. **17**(3), 957–973 (2016)
9. Preissl, R., Wichmann, N., Long, B., Shalf, J., Ethier, S., Koniges, A.: Multi-threaded global address space communication techniques for gyrokinetic fusion applications on ultra-scale platforms. In: Proceedings of 2011 International Conference for High Performance Computing, Networking, Storage and Analysis, pp. 1–11 (2011)
10. Sourcery Institute: Hello-world (2022). https://github.com/sourceryinstitute/hello-world
11. Sourcery Institute (2022). https://github.com/sourceryinstitute/dag
12. Bauer, L., Grudnitsky, A., Shafique, M., Henkel, J.: PATS: a performance aware task scheduler for runtime reconfigurable processors. In: 2012 IEEE 20th International Symposium on Field-Programmable Custom Computing Machines, pp. 208–215. IEEE (2012)
13. Basilio, B., Fraguela, B.B., Andrade, D.: The new UPC++ DepSpawn high performance library for data-flow computing with hybrid parallelism. In: International Conference on Computational Science (2022)
14. Song, F., YarKhan, A., Dongarra, J.: Dynamic task scheduling for linear algebra algorithms on distributed-memory multicore systems. In: Proceedings of the Conference on High Performance Computing Networking, Storage and Analysis, pp. 1–11. IEEE (2009)
15. Cann, D.: Retire Fortran? A debate rekindled. Commun. ACM **35**(8), 81–89 (1992)
16. Dijkstra, E.W.: How do we tell truths that might hurt? ACM Sigplan Notices **17**(5), 13–15 (1982)

17. Kedward, L.J., et al.: The state of fortran. Comput. Sci. Eng. **24**(2), 63–72 (2022)
18. Ehlert, S., et al.: Fortran package manager. In: International Fortran Conference 2021, Zurich, Switzerland, hal-03355768, v1 (2021). https://hal.archives-ouvertes.fr/hal-03355768
19. Austin, B., et al.: NERSC-10 Workload Analysis (2020). https://doi.org/10.25344/S4N30W
20. Fanfarillo, A., Burnus, T., Cardellini, V., Filippone, S., Nagle, D., Rouson, D.: OpenCoarrays: open-source transport layers supporting coarray Fortran compilers, In: Proceedings of the 8th International Conference on Partitioned Global Address Space Programming Models, pp. 1–11 (2014)
21. Singleterry, R. C., et al.: OLTARIS: on-line tool for the assessment of radiation in space. In: NASA/TP-2010-216722 (2010). http://oltaris.nasa.gov

Scalability of Gaussian Processes Using Asynchronous Tasks: A Comparison Between HPX and PETSc

Alexander Strack[(✉)] [iD] and Dirk Pflüger [iD]

Institute of Parallel and Distributed Systems, University of Stuttgart,
70569 Stuttgart, Germany
{alexander.strack,dirk.pflueger}@ipvs.uni-stuttgart.de

Abstract. Gaussian processes are a widely used alternative to neural networks for non-linear system identification. The method requires computing the inversion of a large covariance matrix. In this work, we introduce our new task-based asynchronous implementation, focusing on its most popular solver, the Cholesky decomposition. Our implementation is based on HPX, utilizing its asynchronous many-task runtime system. We can therefore investigate its scaling on multi-core hardware and for GPU offloading. Furthermore, we compare our HPX implementation against a high-level reference implementation based on PETSc. We demonstrate that the HPX implementation's performance is directly tied to the chosen tile size. Compared to the PETSc reference, our task-based implementation is faster in the entire node-level strong scaling experiment on EPYC ROME, showing better parallel efficiency.

Keywords: Asynchronous many-task systems · HPX · PETSc · Tiled Cholesky decomposition · Gaussian processes

1 Introduction

Conventional parallel implementations based on message-based execution models like MPI rely on global synchronization barriers. These barriers can become major performance bottlenecks in complex applications such as coupled numerical simulations or system identification (SI) in control theory [20]. Barriers can be typically found at least at the end of each sub-task, neglecting that some down-stream computations could have already started based on partially available data. We, therefore, study a promising alternative, asynchronous many-task execution models.

Our application is non-linear system identification with Gaussian processes (GPs). This method, employed frequently in control theory [13], aims to build a surrogate of a real-world system with a black-box approach. In other words, no knowledge about the underlying problem can be assumed, but the problem can be run for different parameter settings. Learned from that data, a computed surrogate can then make predictions about the real system. This work, in

P. Diehl et al. (Eds.): WAMTA 2023, LNCS 13861, pp. 52–64, 2023.
https://doi.org/10.1007/978-3-031-32316-4_5

particular, compares two GP implementations. One based on the asynchronous execution model HPX [12] and one based on the widely used PETSc library [2].

Although linear algebra libraries exist that use shared-memory parallelization (see Sect. 2), we choose PETSc as it provides a large variety of functionalities. It includes not only sparse and dense data structures and corresponding linear algebra routines but also iterative solvers that are essential for many applications. The rich feature set, easy-to-use high-level API, and MPI parallelization make PETSc a reference tool in the scientific computing community.

Our main contributions in this work include:

- A new, fully asynchronous task-based implementation of a GP prediction using HPX and multiple different tiled algorithms,
- A reference implementation using PETSc's KSP solver,
- A performance investigation of the tiled algorithms for different tile sizes on multi-core systems and GPU offloading,
- A thorough comparison between the HPX and PETSc implementations in a node-level strong scaling test on a dual socket AMD EPYC 7742 CPU.

The remainder of this work is structured as follows. In the next section, we present related work considering GPs, HPX, and linear algebra libraries. Section 3 describes the scientific application and derives the basics of GPs for SI. We describe the numerical algorithms in Sect. 4, discussing tiled versions of the Cholesky decomposition. Information about the software frameworks we use for the implementations is provided in Sect. 5. The results of our work, including different scaling plots, can be found in Sect. 6. In Sect. 7, we then conclude and give an outlook on future research.

2   Related Work

In contrast to linear SI, the surrogate in non-linear SI does not live on a hyperplane, but a high-dimensional manifold [20]. This property makes the problem much more complex and machine learning methods attractive. Most approaches in literature use either neural networks (NNs) [5,18] or GPs [14,19]. One advantage of GPs is that they contain a built-in uncertainty measure. However, making predictions for unseen data requires computing the inverse of a covariance matrix dependent on the training set size, which can quickly become very expensive. In contrast to sparse matrix approaches [22], which try to reduce the matrix size, we focus on computing the inverse in parallel as fast as possible.

Therefore, we use tiled algorithms and a task-based asynchronous execution model. Several different asynchronous many-task runtimes exist, and a general taxonomy is provided in [21]. In this work, we focus on HPX [12]. Applications of HPX include the astrophysics simulation code Octo-Tiger [15] that enables the simulation of star mergers. There already exist linear algebra libraries that support task-based parallelization. The PLASMA [7] library is currently the reference and uses OpenMP tasks for a shared-memory parallelization of dense linear algebra. Like our approach, it is based on quadratic tiles. On the other hand, the LASs and sLASs [23] libraries provide dense and sparse linear algebra routines. Both take advantage of the OmpSs runtime system. Considering distributed libraries, there is SLATE [9], which provides dense routines with the help of OpenMP tasks and MPI. Furthermore, there is the C library Chameleon [1] developed at Inria. It supports different runtime systems and has distributed capabilities by using StarPU.

3   Scientific Application

For this work, we choose non-linear SI with GPs as an application. The next two subsections introduce the basics of GPs and how they are adapted to a concrete SI application.

3.1   Gaussian Processes

This subsection contains a short introduction to GPs. For more advanced theory, we refer to the book of Kocijan [14]. The general problem is formulated as a blackbox approach where the objective is to learn a non-linear function f. Learning in this context refers to the construction of a surrogate given data that is noisy, e.g., caused by measurement errors. Only a so-called feature matrix

$$Z = [\mathbf{z}_1, \mathbf{z}_2, \dots, \mathbf{z}_N]^T \tag{1}$$

containing N feature vectors $\mathbf{z}_i \in \mathbb{R}^D$ and the corresponding noisy observations

$$\mathbf{y} = [y_1, y_2, \dots, y_N]^T, \; y_i \in \mathbb{R}, \tag{2}$$

are provided as information to learn the function. There are several ways to interpret GPs [17]. One is to view a GP as a collection of random variables $f(\mathbf{z}_i)$, that all share a joint Gaussian distribution $f(\mathbf{z}_i) \sim \mathcal{N}(0, K)$. Note that here the mean of the distribution is set to zero. In practice, it is often used to incorporate prior knowledge. The GP tries to find a good mapping between the feature matrix and the observations by building the covariance matrix $K \in \mathbb{R}^{N \times N}$ with the feature vectors. Each matrix entry is computed by evaluating two feature vectors with a covariance function. For simplicity, we use the *squared exponential kernel*. It is given by

$$C(\mathbf{z}_i, \mathbf{z}_j) = \nu \cdot \exp\left[-\frac{1}{2l} \sum_{d=1}^{D} (z_{i,d} - z_{j,d})^2\right] + \delta_{ij}\sigma \tag{3}$$

where D is the length of the feature vectors. Observe that this function contains three additional parameters. Those are called hyperparameters. Namely the lengthscale l, the vertical lengthscale ν, and the noise variance σ on the diagonal. They have a crucial influence on the quality of the GP and are typically optimized. The GP can then be used to predict M new observations from unseen data. Therefore, we have to build the joint distribution of the N known and M unknown observations $\hat{\mathbf{y}}$

$$\begin{bmatrix} \mathbf{y} \\ \hat{\mathbf{y}} \end{bmatrix} \sim \mathcal{N} \left(0, \begin{bmatrix} K & K_{Z,\hat{Z}} \\ K_{\hat{Z},Z} & K_{\hat{Z},\hat{Z}} \end{bmatrix} \right). \tag{4}$$

Here, $K_{\hat{Z},\hat{Z}} \in \mathbb{R}^{M \times M}$ is the prior covariance matrix, built with the feature matrix of the unseen data $\hat{Z}$. Whereas $K_{\hat{Z},Z} \in \mathbb{R}^{M \times N}$ is the cross-covariance matrix built with the feature vectors of $\hat{Z}$ and Z. The GP prediction of the new observations is given by the mean of this distribution, which is expressed as

$$\hat{\mathbf{y}} = K_{\hat{Z},Z} K^{-1} \mathbf{y}. \tag{5}$$

In addition, GPs provide a prediction uncertainty based on the variance of the joint distribution. It is given by the diagonal of the posterior covariance matrix $\hat{K}$, which can be computed via

$$\hat{K} = K_{\hat{Z},\hat{Z}} - K_{\hat{Z},Z} K^{-1} K_{Z,\hat{Z}}. \tag{6}$$

Since typically $N > M$, the main bottleneck of the prediction (5) is the inversion of the covariance matrix. Hence, the overall computational complexity is $\mathcal{O}(N^3)$ with a direct solver for computing $K^{-1}\mathbf{y}$. Nevertheless, the common choice is the Cholesky decomposition to compute the Cholesky factor L of the factorized matrix $K = L \cdot L^T$. The big advantage of this approach is that the Cholesky factor can be reused for computing the prediction uncertainty (6). This work focuses on the Cholesky decomposition and only implements a basic GP around it. We set the hyperparameters to the empirical moments of our data, following the moment-based initialization in [3]. With this, we omit the hyperparameter optimization, which is crucial to optimize the prediction accuracy. Note that the *negative-log likelihood* loss function is often used in literature to optimize the hyperparameters [14] that again benefits from the Cholesky decomposition: It maximizes the likelihood of the training data $\mathbf{y}|Z \sim \mathcal{N}(0, K)$ and is given by

$$\mathcal{L}(l, \nu, \sigma) = -\frac{1}{2} \log(|K|) - \frac{1}{2}\mathbf{y}^T K^{-1} \mathbf{y} - \frac{N}{2} \log(2\pi). \tag{7}$$

With the precomputed Cholesky factor L the function evaluation simplifies to

$$\mathcal{L}(l, \nu, \sigma) = -\frac{1}{2} \log \left(\prod_i^N L_{ii}^2 \right) - \frac{1}{2}\beta^T \cdot \beta - \frac{N}{2} \log(2\pi), \tag{8}$$

with $\beta \in \mathbb{R}^N$ being the solution of $L^{-1} \cdot \beta = \mathbf{y}$.

3.2 System Identification

GPs are used in control theory as an alternative to NNs for identifying nonlinear systems. The goal is to predict the system behavior for unseen control inputs based on only a given set of input and output time sequences. By filling the feature vectors with so-called regressors, which contain lagged system states, GPs can be used for SI. For simplicity, we use a *non-linear finite impulse response model* [19]. It only requires the input time sequences as regressors. As a result, the feature vectors have the form

$$\mathbf{z}_i = (\mathbf{u}_{i-D}, ..., \mathbf{u}_i) \tag{9}$$

where the $\mathbf{u}_i$ are the control inputs and D is the number of regressors.

As a concrete example, we consider a system of coupled mass-spring dampers. Through non-linear force profiles in the springs between the masses, non-linearity is introduced into the system. The control input is the force applied to the initial mass, while the observations consist of the position of the final mass. The authors of [18] provide a total of $N = 10^5$ training samples and a test set of size $M = 5000$. To make the Cholesky decomposition more stable, we normalized the input data and standardized the output data.

4   Parallel Algorithms

This section describes the tiled algorithms we use in our task-based implementation. First, we must divide the symmetric and positive semi-definite matrix K into tiles. Since we restrict operations to entire tiles, we can only use quadratic tiles. Hence, dividing N samples equally across T tiles leads to a total of T^2 tiles.

Considering the computational effort, our GP application consists of three main parts:

- Assembly of the covariance matrix K in $\mathcal{O}(N^2)$,
- Cholesky solve of $K \cdot \boldsymbol{\alpha} = \mathbf{y}$ in $\mathcal{O}(N^3)$,
- Matrix-vector multiplication $\hat{\mathbf{y}} = K_{\hat{Z},Z}\boldsymbol{\alpha}$ in $\mathcal{O}(M \cdot N^2)$.

The parallel assembly is trivial. There are no data dependencies, as only read operations are performed on the feature vectors. As a result, the different tiles can be computed embarrassingly in parallel. Since K is symmetric, only the lower triangular tiles need to be assembled. The prediction (5) simplifies, after $\boldsymbol{\alpha} \in \mathbb{R}^N$ is computed, to a parallel matrix-vector multiplication. Like its sequential equivalent, the tiled Cholesky solve algorithm first requires a Cholesky decomposition of the matrix and then a forward and backward substitution with the Cholesky factor. We denote the tile in the k-th row and n-th column as K_{kn}.

4.1   Tiled Cholesky Decomposition

Decomposing the matrix K in parallel requires different BLAS routines operating on the matrix tiles. In total, the algorithm needs four BLAS operations [4]:

- *Cholesky decomposition* (POTRF): $L_{kk} = Cholesky(K_{kk})$,
- *Triangular matrix solve* (TRSM): $L_{kk}^T \cdot L_{mk} = K_{mk}$,
- *Symmetric rank-k update* (SYRK): $K_{mm} = K_{mm} - L_{mk} \cdot L_{mk}^T$,

- *General matrix-matrix multiplication* (GEMM): $K_{mn} = K_{mn} - L_{mk} \cdot L_{nk}^T$.

The algorithm can work in-place to save storage. For pseudocode of the right-looking variant, see Algorithm 1. Two more variants exist, namely the left-looking and top-looking Cholesky algorithms, that only differ by the loop arrangements. For more details, we refer to [8]. A closer look at the illustration in Fig. 1 reveals that performance improvements through parallelism are only gained by triangular solving and updating the remaining lower triangular matrix in parallel. Note that the number of parallel tasks reduces as the algorithm progresses down the sub-matrix. That leads to a decrease in parallel efficiency.

```
for k = 0 to T − 1 do
    K_kk = POTRF(K_kk)
    for m = k + 1 to T − 1 do
        K_mk = TRSM(K_kk, K_mk)
    end
    for m = k + 1 to T − 1 do
        K_mm = SYRK(K_mk, K_mm)
        for n − k + 1 to m   1 do
            K_mn = GEMM(K_mk, K_nk, K_mn)
        end
    end
end
```
Algorithm 1: In-place tiled Cholesky decomposition

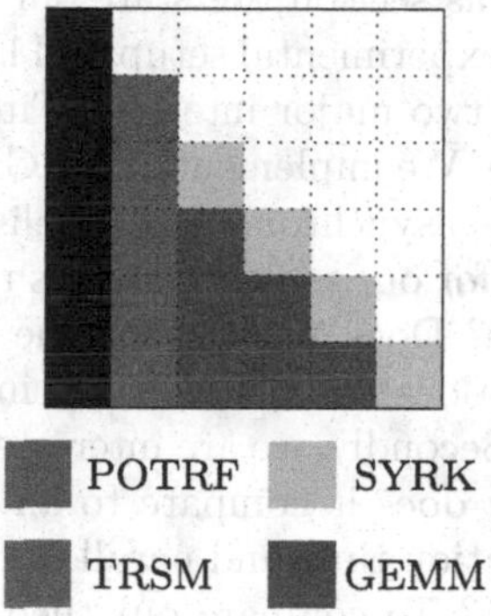

POTRF SYRK
TRSM GEMM

Fig. 1. Tiled Cholesky illustration

In general, for a matrix divided into T^2 tiles, the algorithm executes a total of T POTRF, $\frac{T \cdot (T-1)}{2}$ TRSM and SYRK, and $\frac{T \cdot (T-1) \cdot (T-2)}{6}$ GEMM operations. The most significant impact on the overall performance has the GEMM operation. For example, for $T = 200$, the tiled algorithm executes 200 POTRF, around 20000 TRSM and SYRK, and over a million GEMM operations.

4.2   Tiled Triangular Solve

After computing the Cholesky factor L, it can be used to solve $K^{-1} \cdot y = \alpha$ by first performing a forward substitution $L \cdot x = y$ with the intermediate vector $x \in \mathbb{R}^N$. Then x is used as the right-hand side for the backward substitution $L^T \alpha = x$. The tiled versions of these algorithms require the two BLAS operations

- *triangular vector solve* (TRSV), $L_{kk} \cdot x_k = y_k$, and
- *general matrix-vector multiplication* (GEMV), $y_m = y_m - L_{mk} \cdot x_k$.

Depending on whether forward or backward substitution is used, the operations must be executed on different tiles. The corresponding pseudocode is given in Algorithms 2 and 3. They also work in-place to reduce storage.

for $k = 0$ to $T - 1$ do
   | $\mathbf{y}_k = \text{TRSV}(L_{kk}, \mathbf{y}_k)$
   | for $m = k + 1$ to $T - 1$ do
   | | $\mathbf{y}_m = \text{GEMV}(L_{mk}, \mathbf{y}_k, \mathbf{y}_m)$
   | end
end

Algorithm 2: In-place tiled forward substitution

for $k = T - 1$ to 0 do
   | $\mathbf{y}_k = \text{TRSV}(L_{kk}, \mathbf{y}_k)$
   | for $m = k - 1$ to 0 do
   | | $\mathbf{y}_m = \text{GEMV}(L_{km}^T, \mathbf{y}_k, \mathbf{y}_m)$
   | end
end

Algorithm 3: In-place tiled backward substitution

4.3   Research Questions and Hardware Setup

In this section, we state our main research questions. Furthermore, we describe the experimental setup and hardware we used. The research focus can be divided into two major interests. Firstly, the impact of the tile size on the computation time. We implemented the GP prediction with the help of HPX such that futures allow asynchronous parallelism in the tiled algorithms. What is the optimal tile size for our setup? Can this result be generalized to other hardware and problem sizes? Does outsourcing the matrix update to GPUs improve the performance, and does it impact the optimal tile size?

Secondly, we are interested in the strong scaling of our HPX implementation. How does it compare to an MPI-based implementation regarding overall computation time and parallel efficiency? How do the three main computation parts scale? To compare our tiled algorithms, we used PETSc and implemented the same procedure with the help of the KSP solver. In contrast to setting the tile size ourselves, we let PETSc decide how to partition the matrix. Note that we use PETSc's KSP solver, which was originally intended as an iterative Krylov-subspace method. However, it can perform a Cholesky decomposition by only applying a preconditioner to the matrix.

Considering the hardware setup, we ran our benchmarks on two different systems. The first, which we will refer to as system 1, is a dual socket system containing two AMD EPYC 7742 CPUs with 128 cores combined. The second system consists of one Intel i9-10980XE CPU with 18 cores and one NVIDIA RTX3080 GPU. We will refer to this heterogeneous system as system 2 and use it to investigate the performance of the GEMM offloading.

5   Software Framework

The two main software tools we use are the *High-Performance ParalleX* run-time system [12], short HPX, and the *Portable, Extensible Toolkit for Scientific Computing* [2], short PETSc.

5.1   HPX

HPX, first released in 2008, is a task-based execution model [12]. It is under active development by the STE‖AR Group. Contrary to message-based execution models like MPI, it uses an entirely asynchronous approach that does not rely on global synchronization barriers. By incorporating HPX futures, it is possible to write fully asynchronous code. The HPX source code is almost entirely written in C++, and the API is even C++ standard conform. HPX only provides low-level functionalities and does not directly implement any BLAS routines.

Nevertheless, the Boost library set, an installation prerequisite, comes with *uBLAS*. Although not the best-performing BLAS library, it works out of the box with the HPX wrapper. Furthermore, HPX contains a CUDA executor that allows targeting NVIDIA GPUs [6]. It can access the cuBLAS library of a CUDA installation. To measure the runtimes, we use the APEX library [10]. It can be installed alongside HPX, allowing to time and count annotated function calls.

5.2   PETSc

PETSc, first released in 1995, contains several sparse and dense data structures and routines for scientific computing [2]. As many applications rely on parallelism to be computed in a reasonable time, PETSc uses the MPI standard to handle the necessary communication. It is mainly written in C and is developed by the Argonne National Laboratory. However, it can also be used in C++, Fortran, and even Python code. Due to its extensive functionality and high-level structure, it is part of many scientific computing libraries. The core functionality of PETSc is built around the KSP module. It contains a versatile solver based on preconditioned Krylov-subspace methods. Not all parallel algorithms are part of the standard installation. Thus, we had to configure PETSc to install the *Elemental* library [16] to access the parallel Cholesky preconditioner. A BLAS library in the background handles the numerical computations. PETSc supports different BLAS libraries, but we chose the default option, i.e., *fblaslapack*.

6   Results

The first part of this section discusses the performance impact of the BLAS libraries. Then, we present our results on the influence of different tile sizes. We finally show the node-level strong scaling results and compare the HPX implementation with the PETSc implementation.

Considering the different tiled Cholesky variants, we did not see noticeable performance differences. This observation contrasts the results of [8], where the authors observed significant performance differences using OpenMP on Intel Knights Corner. However, an in-depth investigation of this behavior exceeds the scope of this work. As a result, we only present the runtimes of the right-looking variant (see Algorithm 1). All runtimes are averaged over five runs.

The performance of the BLAS libraries, especially its GEMM operation, is crucial for the overall performance. Recall that the two implementations we compare do not use identical BLAS libraries. Thus, we ran a benchmark comparing the performance of *uBLAS* and PETSc with *fblaslapack* for the relevant operations. For the tile size we used in our strong scaling benchmark, we did not observe a significant performance difference between both libraries. Note that the performance of both implementations could be improved by using faster BLAS libraries, e.g., MKL [11]. If the BLAS operations were directly computed on a GPU using *cuBLAS*, a significant performance advantage can be expected. However, a substantial overhead is introduced by offloading the matrix update to the GPU: Each GEMM operation requires to transfer three matrix tiles to the GPU and one matrix tile back to the CPU. As a result, the performance of the *cuBLAS*-based GEMM operation decreases for shrinking tile size. Here, we focus on a first proof-of-concept considering GPU offloading. In a real-world application, the tile size would have to be optimized for each GPU architecture.

6.1   Tile Scaling

In Fig. 2, the performance of the task-based implementation is illustrated for different tile sizes. We set the accuracy to single precision and choose a problem size of $N = 20000$ and $M = 5000$. The first interesting observation is that the runtime is higher for two tiles per dimension than for the single-tile sequential algorithm. The overhead is introduced by splitting a single sequential BLAS operation on the whole matrix into four but strictly sequential BLAS operations. Parallelism is introduced starting at more than two tiles per dimension. This then leads to significant performance improvements for $T > 2$. Systems 1 and 2 perform about equally well for 16 cores and 18 cores, respectively. Using all 128 cores on system 1 results in much better performance. Choosing a too-small tile size cripples the performance. This becomes visible at $T = 500$, where the overall performance is the same for 16 and 128 cores. Here, the dual socket architecture of System 2 acts as a bottleneck, resulting in bad parallel efficiency.

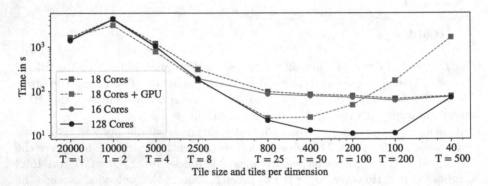

Fig. 2. Tile scaling comparison on two different systems. The workload size is $N = 20000$ and $M = 5000$. Furthermore, all computations are in single precision. Runtimes of system 1, consisting of a dual socket AMD EPYC 7742 with 128 cores, are illustrated with circles. Squares plot system 2 runtimes, which consists of an 18-core Intel i9-10980XE and an NVIDIA RTX3080.

Adding the GPU to system 2 significantly improves the performance and allows it to compete with the 128 cores of system 1 up to 25 tiles per dimension. The runtime increase for larger T has two reasons. First, GPUs require larger workloads to leverage the advantages of their massively parallel architecture. Second, the offloading requires the transfer of four complete matrix tiles per operation. As a result, the optimal tile size for GPU use would be larger.

6.2   Strong Scaling Comparison

For the strong scaling benchmark of the HPX and the PETSc implementation, we again choose a workload size of $N = 20000$ and $M = 5000$. Furthermore, we set the accuracy of the task-based implementation to double precision. Based on the results of the previous subsection, we set $T = 200$, resulting in a tile size of 100×100. Figure 3 shows the total runtime and the different computation blocks' runtimes. The assembly and prediction can be neglected as the Cholesky solve contributes nearly 92% to the total computation time. Across all cores, the task-based implementation has a slight performance advantage. Considering the corresponding parallel efficiency in Fig. 4, both implementations have the same tendency due to hardware limitations. The efficiency drops significantly from 32 to 128 cores. Nonetheless, the efficiency of the HPX implementation is higher and nearly optimal for up to four cores. Finally, performing the benchmark in single precision results in faster runtime for 64 and 128 cores of up to 15% and better efficiency than double precision.

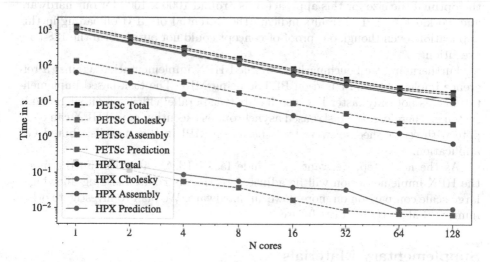

Fig. 3. Node-level strong scaling comparison between the HPX and PETSC implementation on a dual socket AMD EPYC 7742 with 128 cores. The tile size was set to 100×100 for a workload size of $N = 20000$ and $M = 5000$. Both implementations use double precision.

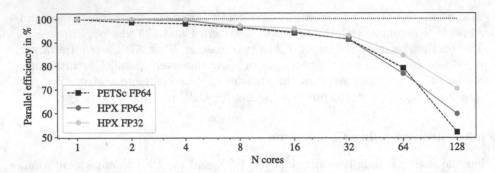

Fig. 4. Parallel efficiency of the strong scaling benchmark in Fig. 3 for the whole application with both PETSc and HPX in double precision. For comparison, we additionally show the results with HPX in single precision.

7 Conclusion and Outlook

We have investigated the scaling and performance impact of the tile size for a tasked-based asynchronous Cholesky decomposition in a GP prediction. In our benchmarks, the optimal tile size on CPUs was around 100×100. However, whether this result can be generalized to bigger workloads remains open. Offloading the GEMM operations to a GPU with the CUDA executor integrated into HPX resulted in a noticeable performance improvement. Due to data transfers, the optimal tile size for this approach was around 1000×1000 for our hardware and workload size. The results indicate the potential of GPU offloading in this application, even though our proof-of-concept could not outperform the 128-core execution.

Furthermore, we benchmarked our tiled HPX implementation against a reference implementation based on PETSc using MPI. The task-based implementation was not only faster but also had better parallel efficiency on single-node systems. Therefore, the task-based asynchronous execution model HPX can compete with established software tools based on MPI in this non-distributed GP application.

As the next step, we want to include faster BLAS libraries. Furthermore, the HPX implementation will be adjusted to the distributed setting allowing a large-scale comparison on more powerful hardware. We plan to investigate other numerical algorithms in the future.

Supplementary Materials

The source code and benchmark data are available at Zenondo. Both implementations contain build scripts that allow the reproduction of our results using identical software versions. We use the GCC compiler at version 9.4.0 for our direct PETSc and HPX comparison.

References

1. Agullo, E., et al.: Achieving High Performance on Supercomputers with a Sequential Task-based Programming Model. Research report, Inria Bordeaux (2016)
2. Balay, S., et al.: PETSc, the portable, extensible toolkit for scientific computation. Argonne National Laboratory, vol. 2 (1998)
3. Basak, S., Petit, S., Bect, J., Vazquez, E.: Numerical issues in maximum likelihood parameter estimation for Gaussian process interpolation. In: Nicosia, G., et al. (eds.) Machine Learning, Optimization, and Data Science. LNCS, vol. 13164, pp. 116–131. Springer, Cham (2022). https://doi.org/10.1007/978-3-030-95470-3_9
4. Buttari, A., et al.: A class of parallel tiled linear algebra algorithms for multicore architectures. Parallel Comput. **35**, 38–53 (2009)
5. Chen, S., Billings, S.A., Grant, P.M.: Non-linear system identification using neural networks. Int. J. Control **51**(6), 1191–1214 (1990)
6. Daiß, G., et al.: Beyond fork-join: integration of performance portable Kokkos kernels with HPX. In: 2021 IEEE IPDPSW, pp. 377–386 (2021)
7. Dongarra, J., et al.: Plasma: parallel linear algebra software for multicore using OpenMP. ACM Trans. Math. Softw. **45**(2), 1–35 (2019)
8. Dorris, J., Kurzak, J., Luszczek, P., YarKhan, A., Dongarra, J.: Task-based cholesky decomposition on knights corner using OpenMP. In: Taufer, M., Mohr, B., Kunkel, J.M. (eds.) High Performance Computing. LNCS, vol. 9945, pp. 544–562. Springer, Cham (2016). https://doi.org/10.1007/978-3-319-46079-6_37
9. Gates, M., et al.: Slate: design of a modern distributed and accelerated linear algebra library. In: SC 2019. Association for Computing Machinery (2019)
10. Huck, K., et al.: An autonomic performance environment for exascale. Supercomput. Front. Innov. **2**, 49–66 (2015)
11. Intel: Intel math kernel library (2023). https://www.intel.com/content/www/us/en/developer/tools/oneapi/onemkl.html
12. Kaiser, H., et al.: HPX - the C++ standard library for parallelism and concurrency. J. Open Source Softw. **5**(53), 2352 (2020)
13. Kocijan, J.: Gaussian process models for systems identification (2008)
14. Kocijan, J.: Modelling and Control of Dynamic Systems Using Gaussian Process Models. Springer, Cham (2016). https://doi.org/10.1007/978-3-319-21021-6
15. Marcello, D.C., et al.: Octo-Tiger: a new, 3D hydrodynamic code for stellar mergers that uses HPX parallelization. Mon. Notices Royal Astron. Soc. **504**(4), 5345–5382 (2021)
16. Poulson, J., et al.: Elemental: a new framework for distributed memory dense matrix computations. ACM Trans. Math. Softw. **39**(2), 1–24 (2012)
17. Rasmussen, C., Williams, C.: Gaussian Processes for Machine Learning. Adaptive Computation and Machine Learning. MIT Press (2006)
18. Revay, M., Wang, R., Manchester, I.: A convex parameterization of robust recurrent neural networks. IEEE Contr. Syst. Lett. **5**, 1363–1368 (2021)
19. Särkkä, S.. The Use of Gaussian Processes in System Identification. In: Balllleul, J., Samad, T. (eds.) Encyclopedia of Systems and Control, pp. 1–10. Springer, London (2019). https://doi.org/10.1007/978-1-4471-5102-9_100087-1
20. Schoukens, J., Ljung, L.: Nonlinear system identification: a user-oriented road map. IEEE Control Syst. **39**, 28–99 (2019)
21. Thoman, P., et al.: A taxonomy of task-based technologies for high-performance computing. In: Wyrzykowski, R., Dongarra, J., Deelman, E., Karczewski, K. (eds.) PPAM 2017. LNCS, vol. 10778, pp. 264–274. Springer, Cham (2018). https://doi.org/10.1007/978-3-319-78054-2_25

22. Titsias, M.: Variational learning of inducing variables in sparse Gaussian processes. J. Mach. Learn. Res. Proc. Track **5**, 567–574 (2009)
23. Valero-Lara, P., et al.: sLASs: a fully automatic auto-tuned linear algebra library based on OpenMP extensions implemented in OmpSs (LASs library). J. Parallel Distrib. Comput. **138**, 153–171 (2020)

Scheduling Many-Task Applications on Multi-clouds and Hybrid Clouds

Shifat P. Mithila[1] , Peter Franz[2] , and Gerald Baumgartner[2]([⊠])

[1] Agricultural Center, Louisiana State University, Baton Rouge, LA 70803, USA
smithila@agcenter.lsu.edu
[2] Division of Computer Science and Engineering, Louisiana State University,
Baton Rouge, LA 70803, USA
{pfranz1,gb}@lsu.edu

Abstract. A centralized scheduler can become a bottleneck for placing the tasks of a many-task application on heterogeneous cloud resources. We have previously demonstrated that a decentralized vector scheduling approach based on performance measurements can be used successfully for this task placement scenario. We then extended this approach to task placement based on latency measurements. Each node collects the performance measurements from its neighbors on an overlay graph, measures the communication latency, and then makes local decisions on where to move tasks. Our recent experiments in CloudLab with nodes allocated on multiple cloud sites demonstrate that using latency in our vector scheduling approach results in better performance and resource utilization. While our algorithm for configuring the overlay graph based on latency measurements was beneficial with simulated communication delays, it was not beneficial in the multi-cloud environment.

Keywords: Many-task computing · Decentralized scheduling · Cloud middleware

1 Introduction

As scientific fields as diverse as quantum chemistry or astrophysics continue to develop, the demand for computational power increases. Historically, researchers have run such applications on clusters or supercomputers. For computational needs beyond what is available at a single university, supercomputer grids and large-scale desktop grids have been developed for certain types of applications. In the last decade, cloud computing has become available as a commercial alternative that allows researchers to rent their computing needs instead of dealing with the expense of purchasing and maintaining a supercomputer.

While it is possible to rent a cluster from a cloud provider, the cheapest resources that can be rented are virtual resources. However, the use of virtualization makes a set of virtual machines behave like a heterogeneous cluster with varying compute performance of the nodes and varying throughput and

P. Diehl et al. (Eds.): WAMTA 2023, LNCS 13861, pp. 65–78, 2023.
https://doi.org/10.1007/978-3-031-32316-4_6

latency of the network connections. Applications with course-grain parallelism, such as MapReduce [9] or graph-parallel algorithms [26] work well in a virtualized environment. However, applications that rely on frequent node-to-node communication or fine-grained parallelism, such as linear algebra code, do not work well with virtual resources

An efficient method for utilizing supercomputer resources is to structure an application as a many-task application [20]. In this approach, an application is broken up into a large number of smaller tasks that are then scheduled. For an early example, Rajbhandari et al. [21] have structured a tensor contraction equation from quantum chemistry as a task graph with dependencies and successfully scaled the application to over 250,000 cores.

We argue that for running a many-task application with fine-grained parallelism in the cloud, it is necessary to identify the performance characteristics of the cloud nodes and their network connections and to map the performance requirements of the tasks onto nodes with matching performance characteristics. E.g., for efficiently running a distributed matrix multiplication algorithm in the cloud it is important that all the nodes that participate in that matrix multiplication have similar performance and low latency connections between them. In a large system, however, collecting the performance information and scheduling tasks on nodes based on that performance information can become very expensive and could cause a centralized task scheduler to become a bottleneck.

This bottleneck of a central scheduler can be eliminated by decentralizing part or all of the scheduling functionality. In IBM's Air Traffic Control (ATC) algorithm [2] decentralized schedulers (air traffic controllers) are directing tasks from a central job queue to the worker nodes. This approach decentralizes the scheduling decisions based on performance information, but it leaves the central job queue as a potential bottleneck. The Organic Grid [5,6] is a fully decentralized approach, in which nodes forward tasks to their neighbors in an overlay network. However, it was designed as a desktop grid infrastructure that assumed unreliable networks, which made the scheduling algorithm too complex and expensive for cloud scheduling.

Peterson et al. [18,19] developed a lightweight fully decentralized task scheduling algorithm for the cloud. In this approach, each node maintains a tasks queue and decides where to migrate extraneous tasks based on performance measurements of its neighbors in an overlay network. In their approach, scheduling decisions are made based on the queue length and the compute performance of each node. Their experiments, however, were simplistic and did not take communication aspects into consideration.

Mithila and Baumgartner [15,16] generalized Peterson et al.'s approach to include latency information, both in the construction of the overlay network and for making scheduling decisions. Their experiments were carried out in a single cloud site and relied on simulated communication delays. In this paper, we report on our recent experiments in a cloud environment with multiple cloud sites and a combination of physical and virtual compute resources. We report on what works, what does not work, and what future research is necessary to achieve the goal of running realistic many-task applications in multi-clouds and hybrid clouds. In particular, we were able to show that it is beneficial to use latency in making scheduling decisions. However, using latency in the overlay graph construction was not beneficial for the particular cloud resources we used.

The rest of the paper is organized as follows: We discuss our decentralized cloud scheduling approach and a summary of our previous experiments in Sect. 2. The results of our new multi-cloud experiments are presented in Sect. 3. Section 4 reviews prior work in the literature. Finally, we conclude the paper and discuss future work in Sect. 5.

2 Decentralized Cloud Scheduling Approach

2.1 Overlay Graph Construction

Peterson et al. used performance measurements of individual nodes to develop a vector-based task scheduling algorithm to optimize overall computation. As the initial network, they used a random graph with 20% connectivity produced with the Erdős-Rényi algorithm. This random construction results in connections that are a combination of slower and faster links.

We intend to generate a better initial overlay graph by utilizing communication information between the nodes. If successful, this would result in better work allocation from the beginning of the experiment. Our assumption is that an overlay graph that reflects the physical architecture, i.e., the distances between nodes, should result in better performance. We start with a full graph and use latency information to drop slower and more distant links. In this process, the experiment controller creates a full graph and sends it to all the worker nodes. Each worker node, upon receiving information about all other nodes, collects their latency measurements and sends them back to the controller. Then the controller, uses a *Hierarchical Clustering* algorithm to group the worker nodes according to the communication distances between them. Each individual cluster has a larger number of connections between the nodes, while there are fewer connections in the overlay graph between distant clusters.

Mithila and Baumgartner [16] presented an overlay graph construction algorithm in which each cluster of nodes forms a clique and in which only 50% of the connections are maintained between a pair of distant clusters. Figure 1 shows an example of how nodes are connected in this graph. In their experiments with simulated communication delays between the clusters, this graph construction algorithm resulted in improved overall performance compared to a random overlay graph.

2.2 Three-Dimensional Vector Scheduling

In our vector scheduling approach, each node advertises its task queue length, its measured performance, and its communication latency to each of its neighbors in the overlay graph. Each node then normalizes the measurements for its neighbors

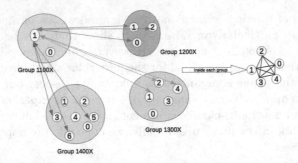

Fig. 1. Connection pattern in our proposed centralized graph construction.

in a $[-1.0, 1.0]$ interval for each dimension and forwards tasks to neighbors in the desired direction. E.g., a node might send tasks to neighbors with shorter queue length, higher performance, and low communication latency.

Mithila and Baumgartner added latency to the scheduling vector along with the neighbors' queue lengths and performance. That is, instead of using two-dimensional (2D) vector scheduling for work distribution as in Peterson et al's work, they designed a three-dimensional (3D) cube with the components queue length, performance, and latency. It is possible to extend this approach to other measurement dimensions.

As an example, an experiment might start with an initial scheduling vector of $[-1.0, 0, -0.5]$, i.e. initially more work will be distributed to the nodes having shortest queue length and some will be distributed to the closer nodes. Then later when about 70% of the work is completed, the scheduling strategy will swap to vector $[-1.0, 0, -0.4]$ i.e., a greater portion of tasks will still be sent to the starving nodes and some tasks will be sent to slightly higher latency nodes while the performance characteristics of nodes do not make any difference.

2.3   Simulated Performance and Latency Variations

For implementation in the cloud, we initially requested a small number of physical machines from a single CloudLab site. In Peterson et al's experiments, as well as in some of Mithila and Baumgartner's experiments, variations in performance were simulated by varying the number of CPU cores available to a given number of worker nodes. Multiple worker nodes are encapsulated inside a Docker container, which is run on varying numbers of CPU cores of the physical machines. For improved repeatability of the experiments, the architectures of the nodes were kept the same.

Since the physical nodes from a single CloudLab clusters are not very distant, Mithila and Baumgartner also introduced artificial communication delays for some of the communication links, such that there are multiple clusters of nodes with low latency within a cluster and higher latency between nodes from different clusters.

To isolate the impact of the additional latency component, variables that could influence performance were minimized or eliminated. To do this, we designed the experiments such that nodes had uniform performance, and that the performance parameter for vector scheduling was kept at zero. Each worker node group is deployed within a docker container. We simulate a situation that worker nodes inside a container portrays nodes situated closely together, so no additional delay is imposed on their links. Groups of nodes inside the same physical machine have some additional delays simulating them slightly more distant from each other, and links to groups in different physical machines have comparatively longer delays to depict them as clusters far from each other. In later experiments, both performance and latency were varied. All of these experiments showed benefits of both the graph construction algorithm that takes latency into consideration and of using latency as one of the dimensions in the vector scheduling algorithm.

2.4   Using Virtual Machines

While using individual sets of cores of physical machines makes the experiments more repeatable, it is not sufficiently realistic. For more realistic experiments, Vannikkarasan varied the task size and introduced communication overhead between tasks [23]. Mithila and Baumgartner then ran additional experiments with these variable loads on a set of virtual machines commissioned from Cloud-Lab.

For virtual machines (VMs) in the cloud, the physical locations of the nodes are not predictable. Therefore, the performance characteristics of virtual nodes and the communication behavior among them can be more unpredictable. For these experiments, each worker node was put into a designated virtual machine.

We requested 47 virtual nodes from the CloudLab Wisconsin site and were given 47 VMs in 10 physical machines of different processor types where the physical nodes consisted of different numbers of VMs ranging from 2 to 7. We varied the task sizes and types and compared the results between random graphs with scheduling only based on the queue length, random graphs with scheduling based on queue length and performance, and our centralized graph construction algorithm with 3-dimensional vector scheduling.

The experiment results for 13 consecutive runs of each of these three scenarios are shown in Fig. 2. The experiments with the random graph and 2D scheduling (in green) show somewhat better performance than for the random gram and queue length-based scheduling (in red) until about three quarters of the experiment. However, both end up performing similarly in the end. Our centralized graph construction with 3D vector scheduling resulted in a lower overall computation time. The shading in the figure indicates the error bars.

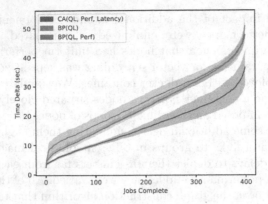

Fig. 2. Experiment results for 13 consecutive runs on VMs comparing a random graph (BP) to our centralized graph construction algorithm (CA) with different scheduling strategies. (Color figure online)

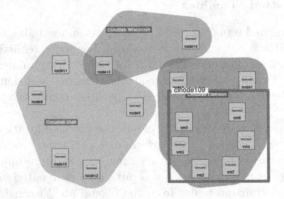

Fig. 3. Cloud node allocation on three sites with physical and virtual machines. (Color figure online)

3   Multi-cloud Experiments

We implemented support in our platform for running experiments that span multiple cloud sites as well as using local machines together with cloud resources. Since our local machines are behind a router with network address translation, which our platform does not handle yet, we simulated a hybrid cloud by using a mix of physical and virtual machines from three different CloudLab [10] sites.

Figure 3 shows our machine configuration with five nodes at CloudLab Utah (in orange), two nodes at CloudLab Wisconsin (in green) and three nodes at CloudLab Clemson (in blue). From the Clemson site, we requested six virtual machines. All of them were allocated in a single physical machine (the blue square). For introducing performance variations, we requested a mix of different architectures for the physical machines.

Because of constraints in getting appropriate resources, we used shorter-running tasks than in our previous experiments and ran most experiment only five times, with a few select experiments ten or 13 times. Each task was a 65×65 matrix multiplication, where one of the argument matrices was shipped as data along with the task to increase the communication overhead, while the other matrix was randomly generated. Each experiment consisted of 400 such tasks and was run on 46 worker nodes. All physical machines we got from CloudLab were configured so that multiple worker nodes on different sets of cores of the same physical machine.

Our experiments demonstrated that our scheduling approach can successfully distribute the tasks for a many-task computation between geographically disjoint computing resources and keep the load on these computing resources reasonably well balanced.

However, because of the large search space of different parameters in our scheduling framework and the characteristics of the available resources, we were not yet able to identify the ideal parameter combinations and to minimize the overall execution time. In this paper, we report on what works, what does not work, and what are promising leads for future work in reducing the overall execution time.

Each experiment consists of four stages:

1. Configuring the overlay graph,
2. Flooding the nodes with tasks,
3. Keeping the nodes busy, and
4. Finishing the last few tasks.

The intuition for the development of our decentralized graph scheduling algorithm was that an overlay graph that reflects the physical distances between the compute node will likely result in improved overall performance, so that, e.g., tasks with large amounts of data do not get sent unnecessarily over long distances. Our experiments with simulated latencies between nodes proved this assumption correct, as shown in Fig. 2.

However, we found that for the multi-cloud experiments using our centralized algorithm for constructing the overlay graph based on latency information resulted in worse performance than using the random graph. One reasons for this is likely that the compute resources we obtained from the different Cloud-Lab sites were not variable enough. Our algorithm assumes that there are various different latencies between groups of nodes, as one would expect from a large commercial cloud provider. The nodes we got from each CloudLab site had very short latencies between them, which suggests that they might have been in the same or in neighboring racks.

Our graph construction algorithm then forms a clique between all neighboring nodes with similar latencies between them. This resulted in the nodes of each CloudLab site forming a clique with too many connections between them, compared to only 20% connectivity for the random graph. It appears that this resulted in tasks being forwarded to new nodes too often before they eventually were executed. For future research, this requires further analysis and tracking

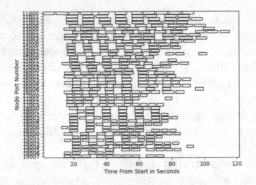

Fig. 4. Sample execution of run emphasizing queue length and ignoring latency.

how often tasks are forwarded between nodes and improvements to our graph construction algorithm.

The next part of the experiment is to ensure that tasks get sent to all nodes as quickly as possible so that the nodes can start computing and do not sit idle in the beginning.

In our previous experiments with 2D scheduling based on queue length and compute performance, it worked best if at the start of the experiment the performance of nodes was disregarded and scheduling was based purely on the queue length.

In our multi-cloud experiments, we found that ignoring latency did not result in good performance and often caused several nodes to be starved at the beginning of the experiment. Figure 4 shows a particularly slow start of the experiment. It used an initial scheduling vector of $[-1, -0.5, 0]$, i.e., a short queue length was emphasized (the first parameter), but performance was considered as well (the second parameter). Most of the best performing runs used a positive latency scheduling parameter, i.e., tasks were pushed away from the local cloud site and were sent across longer latency connections. Figure 5 shows an example of such a run, where the initial scheduling parameters were $[-1, -0.5, 0.5]$, with the third parameter being the latency component.

In these figures, the port numbers identify the individual worker nodes. Each task is indicated by a box. Smaller boxes in a row indicate that this is a faster node. The large gaps at the beginning of the experiment show the time it took for the application to saturate all nodes. The gaps in between tasks show cases where a node was waiting for a task or where a node was slow in communicating.

For the third stage of the experiment, the goal is to keep all nodes busy as long as possible. In our previous 2D scheduling experiments on a single cloud site with simulated performance variations [19], we found that the strategy that worked best was to make scheduling decisions only based on queue length until about 70% of the total running time of the experiment and then to switch to a balanced queue-length and performance strategy. The emphasis on queue length saturated the nodes at the beginning of the experiment as well as kept them

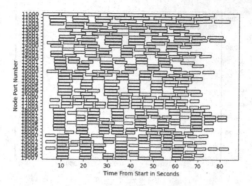

Fig. 5. Sample execution of run considering all three metrics with initial positive (push-away) latency component.

busy later on. For our multi-cloud experiments with latency, especially for the push-away latency parameter, we found that the scheduling strategy needed to be switched no later than about halfway through the experiment. In most of our experiments we switched it after about 30% of the total running time.

During this phase of the experiment, the goal is also to avoid nodes becoming temporarily idle. Ideally, a new task should arrive in the queue just before the previous task completed. Furthermore, we want to avoid tasks from being bounced between nodes multiple times before they are executed. In our previous 2D experiments, concentrating on queue-based scheduling and only having a 20% connectivity in the overlay graph achieved this. Having longer running tasks also helped in reducing gaps caused by waiting for the next task. With latency being a consideration, it is difficult to dial in the scheduling parameters, because there are conflicting goals. Both Figs. 4 and 5 show some larger gaps between tasks, where there is room for improvement.

Towards the end of the experiment, when there are not enough tasks left to keep all nodes busy, it is beneficial to give more emphasis to performance so that the faster nodes execute the remaining tasks. In both figures, the experiment becomes inefficient towards the end, where it takes too long for all the remaining tasks to be executed. In part this is due to not putting enough emphasis on performance, in part it is because more tasks might be left on one of the sites but then are not sent to another site to compute.

What our experiments suggest is that the scheduling parameters should be switched at least twice throughout the experiment, but our platform does not support this yet. Ideally, there should be an initial scheduling strategy that pushes tasks to other sites to ensure that every node gets a task as soon as possible. Then we should give preference to the queue length and migrate tasks primarily within a cloud site to keep all nodes busy while preventing the large communication overhead of shipping tasks back and forth between cloud sites. The final phase should emphasize performance more heavily so the remaining tasks are completed by the fasted nodes, but it also might be necessary to push

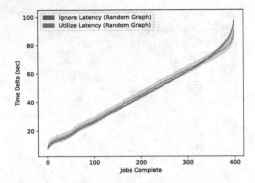

Fig. 6. Performance comparison for multi-cloud experiments. (Color figure online)

tasks to other sites (across high latency links) to balance the tasks between all sites instead of finishing them one site. This switching of the scheduling strategy will need to be performed by an appropriate algorithm. This could be either a decentralized algorithm, where each node makes its own decision on adapting the scheduling vector based on information from its parents, or it could be a centralized algorithm where task completion times are sent to the experiment controller, which then switches the scheduling strategy.

The comparison of two representative sets of experiments in Fig. 6 shows that ignoring latency in scheduling (shown in blue) results in larger job completion times at the end of an experiment. Initially, the differences between the scheduling strategies were not significantly different. Towards the end, however, the strategy that initially emphasized pushing tasks away across links with high latency and that also took latency into consideration at the end of the experiment performed best. For these experiments, we switched the scheduling strategy after 30% of the total running time. While the difference between the scheduling strategies is not large, it is statistically significant. The average over ten runs for ignoring latency (the blue line) was 100.9s, while the average time for using latency as a scheduling parameter was 89.8s. However, for a better comparison, these experiments would need to be repeated for a larger variety of scheduling parameters (including for scenarios where the scheduling strategy is switched twice) and for a larger variety of hardware configurations.

4   Related Work

In traditional grid scheduling [1,22], the meta scheduler focuses on finding an optimal computation schedule given up-to-date and detailed knowledge of the system state. While this approach utilizes resources efficiently, it does not scale to very large numbers of heterogeneous machines or in the presence of unreliable networks.

Desktop grids have been designed as master-worker configurations of machines that are able to scavenge compute resources from a large number of arbitrary machines, even in the pretense of unreliable networks [4,8,14]. While this technology is very mature, it relies on a computational problem to be popular for people to donate their spare compute cycles. E.g., in March 2020, Folding@home, a project aimed as simulating protein dynamics, achieved an aggregate compute power of 1.1 exaFLOPS [25]. However, to prevent the central scheduler (master) from becoming a bottleneck, individual tasks are typically very long running, especially, if they are also data intensive. Furthermore, these systems are designed for independent task applications with no communication between worker nodes.

Cloud computing has become successful as a commercial alternative. Providers offer a variety of services from renting entire clusters to renting sets of virtual machines as well as for specialized purposes, such as file storage. For many applications, MapReduce [9] and graph-parallel algorithms [26] have proved successful, but they are fairly course-grained and do not have frequent communication between cloud nodes. Applications with fine-grained parallelism, such as the NAS MPI benchmarks [24] or atmospheric monitoring programs [11] have not resulted in satisfactory performance, because of the heterogeneity of cloud nodes and the variations in communication latency.

Several approaches have been developed that attempt to schedule fine-grained tasks in the cloud. Luo et al. [13] and Gutierrez-Estevez et al. [12] have proposed fine-grained centralized schedulers that take the application needs into consideration. Mohammadzadeh et al. [17] proposed a centralized scheduling algorithm for a many-task application in which they used multiple objectives for solving scheduling problems.

The Organic Grid demonstrated the feasibility of decentralized scheduling in the context of a desktop grid. As demo applications the authors used the BLAST sequence alignment, an independent task application, as well as a Cannon-style distributed matrix multiplication [5,6]. The algorithms employed in the Organic Grid, however, are too expensive for cloud scheduling. Barsness et al. described the Air Traffic Controller algorithm in an IBM patent [2] that dynamically organizes the worker nodes and results in good performance at the expense of a higher communication overhead for the central job queue and the leader nodes that are organizing the worker nodes.

We argue that for large-scale applications in the cloud with fine-grained parallelism, any centralized schedulers run the risk of becoming a bottleneck, while the decentralized algorithms of the Organic Grid are computationally too expensive. Peterson et al. [18,19] have developed a decentralized vector scheduling approach that used the concept of an overlay network from the Organic Grid, but with a light-weight scheduling algorithm. Mithila and Baumgartner. However, both sets of experiments relied on simulating performance differences and latency differences, respectively. In this paper, we have described our experiments without simulation in a multi-cloud and hybrid cloud environment.

5   Conclusion and Future Work

We have designed a computational platform for running large-scale many-task high-performance applications in the cloud. Because of the heterogeneity of cloud resources, scheduling applications with fine-grained parallelism requires matching the requirements of a task with the performance characteristics of cloud nodes. Since this task scheduling can become a bottleneck for a centralized scheduler, we have proposed a mostly decentralized scheduling approach.

Our scheduling approach relies on an overlay graph for nodes to exchange performance information with neighboring nodes and to send tasks to neighboring nodes. Our previous experiments have used both random graphs and graphs constructed based on latency measurements between pairs of nodes. In our vector scheduling approach, each node collects performance information from its neighbors and decides to which neighbors to send additional tasks.

For making scheduling decisions, a node places its neighbors into a 3D space with the dimensions queue length, performance, and latency and sends tasks to neighbors in the direction of the desired scheduling vector.

We have summarized the experimental results from our prior research and then described our multi-cloud experiments in CloudLab with both physical and virtual nodes from three sites. Our measurements have shown the need for improvements in our scheduling mechanisms. Unlike earlier experiments with simulated latency, the multi-cloud experiments perform best with a random graph, suggesting that our latency-based graph construction algorithm added too many edges to the graph resulting in tasks being migrated unnecessarily. Also, in the multi-cloud experiments the large differences in latency required a different approach to scheduling parameters than for a single cloud site. This indicates the need for an algorithm that adapts the desired scheduling vector as needed during the execution of a many-task application. As an alternative to pushing tasks to nodes, we also plan to experiment with work stealing on the overlay graph, where an idle node steals a task from one of its neighbors.

Our goal is to use our platform for running applications such as the quantum chemistry coupled cluster model for *ab initio* electronic structure modeling [3,21], which is expressible as a tensor contraction equation. Tensor contraction equations, which consist of many compute-intensive generalized matrix multiplications, can be transformed into sets of smaller tasks to be executed as a many-task application.

Tensor contraction equations, however, have additional requirements for our scheduling framework. Instead of a set of tasks, the application is constructed as a task graph with dependencies between the tasks. Furthermore, groups of tasks that are communicating with one another, e.g., for a distributed matrix multiplication, need to be scheduled on neighboring nodes with uniform performance characteristics. And, finally, it will be necessary to take the location of the input data for a task into consideration when migrating a task to another node.

A disadvantage of purely decentralized scheduling is that it can result in longer idle times of nodes in between tasks. We are planning to explore using different performance measurements, corresponding to the dimensions of our scheduling vectors. We will also explore using decentralized scheduling together with some centralized aspects. E.g., the experiment controller could monitor the application and dynamically adjust the scheduling parameters, or the decentralized scheduling approach could consider information from a workflow management system [7].

For a many-task application on a supercomputer, individual tasks can be as short as 200–300 ms. Such a small task granularity would not work in the cloud, since the overhead of sending a task to another virtual machine is too high. On the other hand, if the running time of individual tasks is fairly long, then a centralized scheduler may be more efficient than our decentralized scheduling approach without causing a bottleneck. Additional research is needed for finding the right balance between centralized and decentralized approaches to minimize the task size that can be run efficiently in the cloud.

References

1. Abramson, D., Giddy, J., Kotler, L.: High performance parametric modeling with Nimrod/G: killer application for the global grid? In: Proceedings of 14th International Parallel and Distributed Processing Symposium (IPDPS 2000), pp. 520–528 (2000). https://doi.org/10.1109/IPDPS.2000.846030
2. Barsness, E.L., Darrington, D.L., Lucas, R.L., Santosuosso, J.M.: Distributed job scheduling in a multi-nodal environment. US Patent 8,645,745 (2014)
3. Baumgartner, G., et al.: Synthesis of high-performance parallel programs for a class of ab initio quantum chemistry models. Proc. IEEE **93**, 276–292 (2005)
4. Buaklee, D., Tracy, G., Vernon, M., Wright, S.: Near-optimal adaptive control of a large grid application. In: Proceedings of the 16th International Conference on Supercomputing, pp. 315–326 (2002)
5. Chakravarti, A.J., Baumgartner, G., Lauria, M.: The Organic Grid: self-organizing computation on a peer-to-peer network. IEEE Trans. Syst. Man Cybern.-Part A: Syst. Hum. **35**(3), 373–384 (2005)
6. Chakravarti, A.J., Baumgartner, G., Lauria, M.: Self-organizing scheduling on the Organic Grid. Int. J. High Perform. Comput. Appl. **20**(1), 115–130 (2006)
7. Chen, J., et al.: Beeflow: a workflow management system for in situ processing across HPC and cloud systems. In: 2018 IEEE 38th International Conference on Distributed Computing Systems (ICDCS), pp. 1029–1038 (2018). https://doi.org/10.1109/ICDCS.2018.00103
8. Chien, A., Calder, B., Elbert, S., Bhatia, K.: Entropia: architecture and performance of an enterprise desktop grid system. J. Parallel Distrib. Comput. **63**(5), 597–610 (2003)
9. Dean, J., Ghemawat, S.: Mapreduce: simplified data processing on large clusters. Commun. ACM **51**(1), 107–113 (2008)
10. Duplyakin, D., et al.: The design and operation of CloudLab. In: Proceedings of the USENIX Annual Technical Conference (ATC), pp. 1–14 (2019). https://www.flux.utah.edu/paper/duplyakin-atc19
11. Evangelinos, C., Hill, C.: Cloud computing for parallel scientific HPC applications: feasibility of running coupled atmosphere-ocean climate models on Amazon EC2. Ratio **2**(2.40), 2–34 (2008)

12. Gutierrez-Estevez, D.M., Luo, M.: Multi-resource schedulable unit for adaptive application-driven unified resource management in data centers. In: 2015 International Telecommunication Networks and Applications Conference (ITNAC), pp. 261–268. IEEE (2015)

13. Luo, M., Li, L., Chou, W.: ADARM: an application-driven adaptive resource management framework for data centers. In: 2017 IEEE International Conference on AI & Mobile Services, pp. 76–84 (2017)

14. Maheswaran, M., Ali, S., Siegel, H.J., Hensgen, D., Freund, R.F.: Dynamic mapping of a class of independent tasks onto heterogeneous computing systems. J. Parallel Distrib. Comput. **59**(2), 107–131 (1999)

15. Mithila, S.P.: Scheduling Many-Task Computing Applications for a Hybrid Cloud. LSU doctoral dissertation. 5928, Louisiana State University and Agricultural and Mechanical College (2022)

16. Mithila, S.P., Baumgartner, G.: Latency-based vector scheduling of many-task applications for a hybrid cloud. In: 2022 IEEE 15th International Conference on Cloud Computing (CLOUD), pp. 257–262 (2022). https://doi.org/10.1109/CLOUD55607.2022.00047

17. Mohammadzadeh, A., Masdari, M., Gharehchopogh, F.S.: Energy and cost-aware workflow scheduling in cloud computing data centers using a multi-objective optimization algorithm. J. Netw. Syst. Manag. **29**(3), 1–34 (2021)

18. Peterson, B.: Decentralized Scheduling for Many-Task Applications in the Hybrid Cloud. LSU doctoral dissertation. 4223, Louisiana State University and Agricultural and Mechanical College (2017)

19. Peterson, B., Fazlalizadeh, Y., Baumgartner, G., Wang, Q.: A vector-scheduling approach for running many-task applications in the cloud. In: Luo, M., Zhang, L.-J. (eds.) CLOUD 2018. LNCS, vol. 10967, pp. 3–19. Springer, Cham (2018). https://doi.org/10.1007/978-3-319-94295-7_1

20. Raicu, I., Foster, I.T., Zhao, Y.: Many-task computing for grids and supercomputers. In: 2008 Workshop on Many-Task Computing on Grids and Supercomputers, pp. 1–11. IEEE (2008)

21. Rajbhandari, S., Nikam, A., Lai, P., Stock, K., Krishnamoorthy, S., Sadayappan, P.: A communication-optimal framework for contracting distributed tensors. In: SC 2014: Proceedings of the International Conference for High Performance Computing, Networking, Storage and Analysis, pp. 375–386. IEEE (2014)

22. Taylor, I., Shields, M., Wang, I.: Resource management for the triana peer-to-peer services. In: Nabrzyski, J., Schopf, J.M., Weglarz, J. (eds.) Grid Resource Management, pp. 451–462. Springer, Boston (2004). https://doi.org/10.1007/978-1-4615-0509-9_27

23. Vannikkarasan, H.: Decentralized scheduling in cloud with variable size tasks. Technical report, Louisiana State University (2021)

24. Walker, E.: Benchmarking Amazon EC2 for high-performance scientific computing. Mag. USENIX SAGE **33**(5), 18–23 (2008)

25. Wikipedia: Grid computing (2023). https://en.wikipedia.org/wiki/Grid_computing

26. Xin, R., Gonzalez, J., Franklin, M., Stoica, I.: Graphx: a resilient distributed graph system on spark. In: First International Workshop on Graph Data Management Experiences and Systems, pp. 1–6 (2013)

Author Index

Printed in the United States
by Baker & Taylor Publisher Services

Printed in the United States
by Baker & Taylor Publisher Services